THE ROLE OF FINANCIAL MARKETS IN GENERATING BUSINESS CYCLES

THE ROLE OF FINANCIAL MARKETS IN GENERATING BUSINESS CYCLES

Luca Matteo Stanca

Mellen Studies in Economics
Volume 11

The Edwin Mellen Press
Lewiston•Queenston•Lampeter

Library of Congress Cataloging-in-Publication Data

Stanca, L. M. (Luca Matteo)
The role of financial markets in generating business cycles / Luca Matteo Stanca.
p. cm. -- (Mellen studies in economics ; v. 11)
Includes bibliographical references and index.
ISBN 0-7734-7357-2
1. Business cycles. 2. Investments--Decision making. I. Title. II. Series.

HB3711 .S718 2002
338.5'42--dc21

2001044018

This is volume 11 in the continuing series
Mellen Studies in Economics
Volume 11 ISBN 0-7734-7357-2
MSEc Series ISBN 0-7734-7966-X

A CIP catalog record for this book is available from the British Library.

The Edwin Mellen Press
Box 450
Lewiston, New York
USA 14092-0450

The Edwin Mellen Press
Box 67
Queenston, Ontario
CANADA L0S 1L0

The Edwin Mellen Press, Ltd.
Lampeter, Ceredigion, Wales
UNITED KINGDOM SA48 8LT

Printed in the United States of America

To my parents

Contents

List of Tables

List of Figures

Preface

This book studies the empirical relation between business cycles, their asymmetries, and the cross-sectional distribution of firms' financial performance. The topic is timely and exciting, with, in reality, ever greater diversity now observed across firms and industries in all countries, as information and communications technologies lead to internal reorganization, and dramatic success and failure occur across and within different industries.

The book's analysis ties in neatly also with frontier theoretical research on monetary policy, credit constraints and capital market imperfections, and aggregate economic fluctuations. The key idea is that the inherent nature of credit market imperfections creates natural asymmetries in business cycles: Downturns are potentially extreme as firms find themselves denied credit, and dramatically reduce investment spending. While other recent studies have attempted to put empirical flesh on these fascinating theoretical ideas, Dr Stanca's research—it seems to me—comes closest to capturing what really matters in their transmission mechanism implications for aggregate economic fluctuations.

Dr Stanca uses a wide range of sophisticated econometric techniques, well-tuned to study asymmetries, nonlinearities, and the dynamics of a rich cross-section distribution. He finds that asymmetries and nonlinearities matter importantly in business cycles, and that aggregate fluctuations are jointly endogenously determined with individual firms' financial conditions. His results also suggest support for capital market imperfections as a transmission mechanism for business cycles.

This book thus contributes importantly to the study of macroeconomic dynamics in two distinct ways: First, it clarifies the limitations of linear analysis in missing many important insights. Second, it jointly models aggregate fluctuations with important microeconomic dynamics, namely that of individual firms' financial situations. In so doing, the book provides an insightful linkage between frontier theoretical ideas and the empirical analysis of aggregate business cycles.

Danny T. Quah
London School of Economics

Acknowledgements

This work has benefited from the comments and suggestions of many people. In particular, I would like to thank Danny Quah, whose advice and suggestions have been most instructive and encouraging. I am indebted to Mauro Gallegati, who helped me to reshape many of the ideas contained in this work. I also would like to thank Charles Bean, Emilio Colombo, Domenico Delli Gatti, Nobu Kiyotaki, Christopher Pissarides, Pierluigi Porta, Lucrezia Reichlin, Francisco Requena, and Andrew Scott. The book is dedicated to my parents.

Chapter 1

Introduction

This book presents the results of an empirical investigation into the nature and causes of aggregate economic fluctuations. The focus of the analysis is on the link between changes in corporate financial positions and asymmetries in macroeconomic fluctuations. In particular, the book addresses two main related topics. First, at the macroeconomic level, we assess the stability of business cycles features over time and the nature and significance of business cycle asymmetries. Second, at the microeconomic level, we investigate the distribution dynamics of firms' financial positions and the dynamic interaction between financial conditions and investment spending. This introduction provides the motivation and a brief outline of the book.

In the last two decades there has been renewed attention among economists for the empirical regularities of aggregate economic fluctuations. Such interest is explained not only by the fact that documenting stylized facts is the natural starting point of scientific analysis, but also by specific developments in the methodology of macroeconomic analysis.

In *Understanding Business Cycles* (1977), Robert Lucas made an important methodological point: understanding aggregate fluctuations means being able to construct model economies that can closely replicate the time series properties of actual economies. Following Lucas, a number of empirical studies have attempted to establish robust *stylized facts* of the business cycle. The resulting time-domain regularities have been taken as a benchmark in the assessment of the empirical validity of appropriately calibrated Real Business

Cycle (RBC) models.[1]

The recent renewed attention for business cycle empirics has also coincided with a significant change in the methods of empirical business cycle analysis. The classical techniques developed by the National Bureau of Economic Research (NBER) treated each cycle as a separate episode, to be analysed explicitly as a sequence of cyclical phases. Having identified a business cycle chronology, researchers would characterize cycles and phases in terms of duration, amplitude, and lead-lag relationships with respect to the reference series. The emphasis on the individuality of cycles and phases is evident in the classic definition of the business cycle provided by Burns and Mitchell (1946):

> "Business cycles are a type of fluctuation found in the aggregate economic activity of nations that organize their work mainly in business enterprises: a cycle consists of expansions occurring at about the same time in many economic activities, followed by similarly general recessions, contractions, and revivals which merge into the expansion phase of the next cycle; this sequence of changes is recurrent but not periodic; in duration business cycles vary from more than one year to ten or twelve years; they are not divisible into shorter cycles of similar character with amplitudes approximating their own." (Burns and Mitchell, 1946, p. 3)

Modern business cycle analysts, however, have departed from the classical methodology, and have thus abandoned the emphasis on individual cycles and phases, adopting instead time series techniques that describe the cyclical behaviour of an economic time series *as a whole*. This shift of emphasis is reflected in the definition of the business cycle adopted by the RBC literature, as exemplified by Prescott (1986):

> "We follow Lucas (1977) in defining business cycle phenomena as the recurrent fluctuations of output about trend and the co-movements among other aggregate time series." (Prescott, 1986, p. 10)

The shift of attention from the properties of individual cycles and phases to the properties of the whole time series reflected two factors. The first was, at the theoretical level, the lack of a statistical foundation for the methods of

[1] See Quah (1995), and the papers therein introduced, for a discussion of different quantitative methods for evaluating business cycle models.

classical business cycle analysis. This was one of the main points raised by Koopmans (1947) in his *Measurement without theory* critique of the NBER methodology. The second factor was, at the empirical level, the widespread acceptance of the assertion, also to be found in Lucas (1977), that business cycles are *all alike*. That is, more precisely, the assumption that the co-movements among aggregate time series present features which are to a large extent systematic across economies and across cycles.[2]

As a result of these methodological developments, the techniques for the descriptive analysis of business cycles have changed. Most of the recent empirical literature describes aggregate fluctuations in terms of time-domain summary statistics.[3] The three traditional business cycle dimensions – amplitude, duration, and co-movements – are characterized by means of standard deviations, auto-correlations, and cross-correlations, respectively. Measuring business cycles in terms of sample second moments, however, may imply a loss of information, as it can hide the different nature and causes of individual cyclical episodes.

Regarding business cycle modelling, modern macroeconometricians typically analyse aggregate fluctuations within the Frisch-Slutsky analytical approach, whereby random shocks (the *impulses*) affect output through distributed lag relations (the *propagation mechanism*).[4] This approach has the substantial advantage of allowing a better integration of macroeconomic theory and econometrics, but it can also lead to a loss of information. In particular, within the Frisch-Slutsky framework it is commonly assumed that the propagation mechanism is linear and that the disturbances follow a gaussian distribution.

Modelling business cycles under the assumption of *linear* propagation mechanism and *gaussian* disturbances imposes a symmetric behaviour over the business cycle, so that asymmetries between expansions and contractions may be overlooked. The existence of systematic business cycle asymmetries,

---

[2] "One is led by the facts to conclude that, with respect to the qualitative behaviour of co-movements among series, business cycles are all alike." (Lucas, 1977, p. 218).

[3] A smaller part of the literature, however, characterizes business cycles in the frequency-domain (see e.g. Sargent and Sims, 1977; Sargent, 1979).

[4] See Blanchard and Fischer (1989), chapter 6, for a historical overview of business cycle modelling.

however, would have a number of important implications. In particular, theoretical business cycle models should incorporate asymmetric behaviour; linear forecasting models which ignore information about the state of the economy would be inefficient; the design and implementation of stabilization policies would have to be conditional on the stage of the cycle. This has spurred in recent years a substantial body of research on testing and modelling business cycle asymmetries. Indeed, Romer (1996) includes *asymmetries in output movements* (in terms of duration) among the stylized facts of short-run fluctuations. While much work has attempted to test for the presence and to characterize the nature of cyclical asymmetries, relatively less work has tried to assess the empirical significance of alternative theoretical interpretations.[5]

One recent interpretation of the presence of cyclical asymmetries at the aggregate level relies on the idea that changes in agents' financial conditions may contribute to amplify and propagate the impact of exogenous shocks to economic activity (see e.g. Bernanke and Gertler, 1989; Greenwald and Stiglitz, 1993; Kiyotaki and Moore, 1997). Asymmetric information in capital markets makes it costly for lenders to evaluate the quality of firms' investment projects, so that the cost of new debt or equity can be substantially higher than the opportunity cost of internal finance. As a consequence, for certain classes of firms investment depends on financial factors such as the availability of internal finance and the access to new debt or equity finance. At the macroeconomic level, this implies that when an adverse shock worsens firms' financial conditions, this negatively affects their internal finance and access to credit, and the resulting decline in investment can thus contribute to amplify the cyclical downswing, through the so-called financial accelerator effect.

Financial accelerator effects can be expected to be stronger the deeper the economy is in a recession, and the weaker the balance sheet of borrowers, since credit constraints are binding across a wider cross section of firms in contractions than in expansions. Although this prediction has found some empirical support (Gertler and Hubbard, 1988; Kashyap *et al.*, 1994; Gertler and Gilchrist, 1994), most empirical tests of financial business cycle theories

[5] See the reviews in Mittnik and Niu (1994), Pfann (1993), and Potter (1994). See also Acemoglu and Scott (1997), Ball and Mankiw (1994), Caballero and Engel (1993) for recent theoretical interpretations of cyclical asymmetries.

rely on firms' heterogeneity, following the approach in the seminal work by Fazzari *et al.* (1988).[6]

Against this background, the objective of this study is twofold. On the one hand, we try to assess at the macro level the validity of the assumption, implicit in most recent empirical analyses of aggregate fluctuations, that business cycle are all alike, and that cyclical phases are alike. Our conclusion is that both the *representative cycle* and the *representative phase* hypotheses can in many cases be rejected. Describing business cycles only in terms of sample second moments, and imposing symmetric behaviour between expansions and contractions, is likely to lead to a substantial loss of information. On the other hand, we try to asses at the micro level the empirical significance of one possible economic interpretation of business cycle asymmetries: the role of changes in agents' financial positions in propagating the impact of shocks. Our conclusion is that the evidence supports the hypothesis that, in the presence of capital market imperfections, agents' financial positions have an important role for aggregate cyclical dynamics.

The book is structured in four parts. Chapter 2 investigates the main features of business cycles in historical perspective, in an attempt to identify the stylized facts to be explained and replicated by theoretical models.[7] The chapter also reconsiders the assumption that business cycles are *all alike*, and complements the time-domain analysis with a classical analysis of individual cycles and phases. We find robust evidence that the amplitude of GDP fluctuations has decreased significantly in the post-war period, and interpret the results as being consistent with the increasing role of stabilization policies. We also provide formal tests, for ten industrialized countries, of various aspects of the hypothesis that business cycles are all alike. The results show that there is substantial heterogeneity in individual cycles and phases in terms of duration, amplitude, and co-movements between variables, and that such heterogeneity is generally statistically significant.

---

[6]The sensitivity of investment spending to changes in financial positions is expected to be higher for firms believed to face significant agency costs. Empirical investigations of financial business cycle theories thus typically split the sample into groups according to a number of criteria thought a-priori to identify financially constrained firms, such as dividend policy, age, size, industrial group, bond rating, stock listing, and ownership structure.

[7]This chapter draws on Stanca (1998, 1999a,b). See also Gallegati and Stanca (1998).

Chapter 3 reports the results of an empirical investigation of business cycle asymmetries in aggregate fluctuations (see Stanca, 1999c). Macroeconomic time series, both long-run annual and post-war quarterly, are investigated to test for the presence of non-linearity and cyclical asymmetry. The dynamics of recessions and expansions are then modelled with threshold autoregressive and Markov-switching models. We show that allowing for two regimes is sufficient to account for the finding of neglected non-linearity. The results indicate that business cycle asymmetries can provide both an intuitive economic interpretation and a parsimonious representation of non-linearities in macroeconomic time series.

Chapter 4 presents an empirical study of the implications of agents' heterogeneity for theories of macroeconomic fluctuations based on the role of financial variables (see Stanca *et al.*, 1999). We apply models of explicit distribution dynamics to company account data for manufacturing firms to investigate the dynamics of the cross-section distribution of firms' financial positions, and its interactions with aggregate activity. We find that the pattern of cyclical co-movements is consistent with models where aggregate fluctuations are endogenously and jointly determined with financial conditions. The dynamics of different parts of the leverage distribution contain significant predictive information for aggregate investment growth. The distribution dynamics reveal substantial intra-distribution mobility, although there is little evidence of significant interactions with aggregate economic activity. Intra-distribution mobility is higher for small than for large firms, and displays asymmetric patterns across business cycle phases.

Chapter 5 investigates the dynamic interaction between financial conditions and investment by estimating and testing vector autoregressions on company account panel data for manufacturing firms (see Stanca and Gallegati, 1999). The results show that indicators of liquidity and solvency contain significant predictive information for investment at firm level. We also find evidence of both cross-sectional and time heterogeneity: the role played by financial factors is significantly more important for highly leveraged than for low-debt firms; capital market frictions are shown to have asymmetric effects, displaying a larger impact in contractions than in expansions. Overall, the evidence supports the hypothesis that capital market imperfections have an important role in explaining aggregate cyclical dynamics.

Chapter 6 concludes by summarizing the main results and the implications for business cycles research.

Chapter 2

The Historical Properties of Macroeconomic Fluctuations

2.1 Introduction

One of the important contributions made by Lucas (1977) to the methodology of business cycle analysis is the following simple idea: understanding aggregate fluctuations means being able to construct model economies which can closely replicate the time series properties of actual economies.[1] Following Lucas (1977), a number of studies tried to establish robust stylized facts of the business cycle, to be used as a benchmark to assess the validity of appropriately calibrated Real Business Cycle (RBC) models. Most of this research was initially concentrated on quarterly post-war data for the U.S. economy (e.g. Prescott, 1986; Kydland and Prescott, 1990), while relatively little evidence was available for other countries and time periods. More recently, a number of studies have extended the analysis both to European countries, while retaining the focus on quarterly post-war data (Danthine and Girardine, 1989; Blackburn and Ravn, 1990; Fiorito and Kollintzas, 1994; Dolado *et al.*, 1993), and to annual long-run data (Backus and Kehoe, 1992; Correia *et al.*, 1990; Englund *et al.*, 1992; Hassler *et al.*, 1994).

As yet, though, there is no comprehensive analysis of economic fluctuations in Italy in a long term perspective. On the one hand, most recent empirical

[1] "One exhibits understanding of business cycles by constructing a model in the most literal sense: a fully articulated artificial economy which behaves through time so as to imitate closely the time series behaviour of actual economies", Lucas (1977), p. 219.

analyses of Italian business cycles either focus exclusively on post-war developments (Ancona and Bonato, 1995; Chiarini, 1994; Pistoresi, 1996; Schlitzer, 1993) or, when taking a long run perspective, adopt a methodological approach which does not account for the heterogeneity of individual cycles and cyclical phases over a long sample period (e.g. Ardeni and Gallegati, 1991, 1994).[2] On the other hand, the analyses of post-unity Italian economic development by economic historians (e.g. Toniolo, 1978; Zamagni, 1993; Fuà, 1981) tend to concentrate more on long term growth and institutional changes than on short term cyclical fluctuations.

The objective of this chapter is therefore to describe and analyse the main features of business cycles in the Italian economy from the unification of the country to the present (1861-1995). The analysis is motivated by the simple idea that it is essential to know precisely what facts one should be able to explain and replicate when developing theoretical models. This chapter, however, also intends to question the assumption implicit in the empirical strategy proposed by Lucas (1977), and later adopted in the RBC literature, that business cycles are *all alike*.[3] Accordingly, we try to go beyond what we refer to as the *representative cycle* hypothesis, by complementing the analysis based on time-domain summary statistics with a classical analysis of individual cycles and cyclical phases. We also provide formal tests, for ten industrialized countries, of various aspects of the representative cycle hypothesis.[4]

The results of the analysis are twofold. First, we provide a small set of time-domain regularities for the Italian economy for the 1861-1995 period, thus extending and qualifying some of the results in the literature. We also examine the evidence on the post-war stabilization of business cycles, and find robust evidence that the amplitude of GDP fluctuations has decreased significantly in the post-war period. Second, we show that there is substantial heterogeneity in specific cycles and phases in terms of duration, amplitude,

[2] Some recent studies, while using long-run Italian time series, concentrate on specific issues such as the representation of the non-stationary component (Caselli and Marinelli, 1994; Gallegati, 1996), the degree of persistence of impulses (Croce, 1996), and the post-war stabilization of fluctuations (Schlitzer, 1995).

[3] "One is led by the facts to conclude that, with respect to the qualitative behaviour of co-movements among series, business cycles are all alike", Lucas (1977), p. 216.

[4] This chapter draws on Stanca (1998, 1999a,b). See also Gallegati and Stanca (1998).

and co-movements between variables, and that such heterogeneity is generally statistically significant.

Overall, our conclusion is that business cycles are not at all alike, and neither are cyclical phases. That is, the univariate features of economic time series and, more importantly, the co-movements among the main economic aggregates, are not qualitatively similar across different cyclical episodes and across cyclical phases. This has implications for both econometric practice and economic theory. At the empirical level, our results suggest that, in order to improve our understanding of economic fluctuations, it is important not to characterize business cycles only in terms of sample second moments: it is also necessary to study the features of specific cycles, and to investigate the differences in the behaviour of economies across cyclical phases. At the theoretical level, our results underline the difficulties of developing theories providing a unified explanation of *the* business cycle. The rejection of the representative cycle hypothesis suggests a research strategy focusing on the interactions between distribution dynamics at the micro level and aggregate fluctuations, an approach which we will follow in chapters 4 and 5.

The chapter is structured as follows. Section 2.2 discusses the data set and the methodology. Section 2.3 presents time-domain empirical regularities for the Italian business cycle. Section 2.4 examines the evidence on the stabilization of post-war macroeconomic fluctuations. Sections 2.5 and 2.6 departs from the *representative cycle* assumption, and provides a description of Italian aggregate fluctuations taking individual cycles and cyclical phases as separate entities, as in the classical approach of the National Bureau of Economic Research (NBER). Section 2.7 presents the results of statistical tests of the hypothesis that business cycles are all alike, and section 2.8 concludes with a summary of the main results and the implications of our findings.

2.2 Data and Methodology

Data limitations have hampered until recently the study of business cycles in Italy in a long-run perspective. Cross-country long run comparisons of macroeconomic fluctuations including the Italian economy (e.g. Sheffrin, 1988;

Backus and Kehoe, 1992) were based on the set of historical data published by the Italian central statistical office (ISTAT, 1957). This data set consisted of retrospective estimates of national product measured at current prices (disaggregated with respect to both use and formation of resources) and at 1938 constant prices (disaggregated with respect to use alone). The ISTAT data set was revised a few years later by a group of researchers at Ancona University (Fuà, 1978). The revised data set (henceforth referred to as *Fuà*) included estimates at constant prices of national product disaggregated also with respect to the formation of resources. The ISTAT and Fuà historical data sets, however, suffer from two major limitations. First, they lead to the much debated conclusion that there has been little or no economic growth in the 1861-1890 period (Toniolo, 1978). Second, they report measures at 1938 constant prices for the entire 1861-1952 period.

A first attempt to solve these problems was made by Maddison (1991), who recalculated the series for value added at constant prices by using the weights of 1870 and 1913 for the 1861-1913 and 1913-1938 periods, respectively.[5] More recently, Rossi *et al.* (1993) reconstructed the whole Italian historical data set by using new estimates for two benchmark years, 1911 and 1951, provided by the Bank of Italy (Rey, 1992) and Golinelli and Monterastelli (1990), respectively. This revised data set is particularly useful, as it is consistent with the overall redefinition of the national accounts made by ISTAT in 1987.[6] In a recent paper Fuà and Gallegati (1996), henceforth FG, underlined the difficulties arising with such data when comparing the products of two years that are relatively close to each other but distant from the year whose prices are chosen as constants. They argued that the measurement is more significant if it is carried out using a system of values prevailing at times closer to the dates to be compared, and proposed a chain index of the Italian GDP to overcome the difficulties deriving from expressing a real long-run time series at constant prices of individual years which are far apart in the sample period.

[5]Maddison used the revised estimates of Fenoaltea (1987) for mines, construction and public consumption in the years 1861-1913 and those of Golinelli and Monterastelli (1990) for the years 1951-1970.

[6]It should be noted, however, that this data set is expressed for the entire sample at constant prices of only two years: 1938 and 1985 for the 1890-1951 and 1951-1992 periods, respectively.

The empirical analysis in this chapter is mainly based on the revised estimates of Rossi *et al.* (1993), for the 1891-1992 period. These series were extended backward, for the 1861-1890 period, on the basis of the Fuà(1978) data set.[7] For the identification of the cyclical chronology and the analysis of the post-war stabilization of fluctuations, we also considered the GDP chain index proposed in Fuà and Gallegati (1996). The Money stock (M2), long term interest rate, budget components, and the wholesale price index are from Fratianni and Spinelli (1997). For the 1981 to 1995 period these series were extended using data from the OECD Analytical Data Bank (ADB) database. Real wages were obtained dividing nominal wages (available only starting in 1893) by the GDP deflator. Labour productivity is given by GDP over the total number of employed, while the Solow residual was calculated assuming constant returns to scale and a constant 0.36 capital share. The latter two variables, as the employment series, are only available starting in 1911. Overall, the resulting historical data set for the Italian economy comprises 29 time series, which can be divided into three groups: GDP and its expenditure components, monetary variables, and labour market variables. The historical data for GDP in the remaining G7 countries are from Maddison (1995) and Mitchell (1993).

The international historical time series analysed in section 2.6 are based on an updated and revised version of the Backus and Kehoe (1992) long run international data set. The original data set consists of annual observations in the 1850-1986 interval for real GDP, Investment, Private Consumption, Public Consumption, Net exports, Money stock, and the GDP deflator for 10 industrialized countries (Australia, Canada, Denmark, Germany, Italy, Japan, Norway, Sweden, United Kingdom, United States).

The original data set was updated and integrated using a number of different sources. All series were extended to 1996 by means of the corresponding OECD Main Economic Indicators (MEI) variables. The observations for the war years for the GDP of Denmark, Germany, Japan, and Norway were ob-

[7]The series were also extended forward from 1992 to 1995, where necessary, using the corresponding series from the OECD MEI-ADB data bases. Splices between the series were obtained, as in Backus and Kehoe (1992), by multiplying the earlier series by a constant, chosen so that both series take the the same value at the splice point.

tained from the corresponding estimates of Maddison (1995). The missing series for Australia, Canada, and Germany were obtained from the corresponding series in Liesner (1989). The series for Italy were replaced by the estimates of Rossi *et al.* (1993) for 1891-1992, and of Fuà (1978) for the 1861-1890 period.

In order to analyze business cycle regularities it is necessary to identify an appropriate measure of the cyclical component. This poses a number of problems. First, at the empirical level, there is no fully satisfactory statistical technique for decomposing time series into cyclical and trend components. Detrending procedures may transpose cycles, induce artificial cycles, or lead to overestimate fluctuations. More generally, different detrending techniques can produce different - and in some cases spurious - stylized facts (see Canova, 1998, 1999; Cogley and Nason, 1995).[8] Second, at the theoretical level, cyclical and secular movements are likely to be interdependent (see the survey in Saint-Paul, 1997). Many authors have argued that, because cycle and trend are inextricably linked, it is meaningless to make any distinction at all.

In recognising the force of these criticisms, and in particular the view that similar forces affect both trend and cycle, this paper relies on two decomposition techniques: the Hodrick-Prescott (HP) filter[9] and first order differencing. These filters present the main advantage of ease of comparability with previous studies (for an assessment of the robustness of business cycle features to different detrending methods see Stanca, 1996). In addition, from a theoretical perspective, these techniques are intended to reflect two opposite views of macroeconomic fluctuations.

At one extreme is the idea, shared by Schumpeter (1939), Kaldor (1954), and Goodwin (1955), that business cycles are an intrinsic element of the growth process, and that an integrated theory of cyclical economic growth is thus required.[10] In this view the growth process is itself cyclical, and the

[8]See also the recent literature on the use of band pass filters to extract cyclical fluctuations (Baxter and King, 1995, Guay and St-Amant, 1997; Hassler *et al.*, 1994; Stock and Watson, 1998).

[9]There is an abundant literature on the properties of this Whittaker-Henderson filter, originally introduced to the economics literature by Hodrick and Prescott (1980). One of the best references is probably King and Rebelo (1993).

[10]This is also the view of Real Business Cycle (RBC) theorists. In this respect, it is ironic

business cycle is naturally identified with observed movements in the growth rate of economic activity. At the other extreme is the idea that growth and business cycles are separately identifiable phenomena, and thus can be treated theoretically as unrelated areas of macroeconomic analysis. Within this view, it appears natural to identify and analyze separately the long-run (growth) and the short-run (cyclical) components. The HP filter is then just one of the many possible decomposition techniques, made particularly appealing by its flexibility and ease of comparability. As the filter was applied to annual data, we followed Backus and Kehoe (1992) in setting the penalization coefficient (λ) equal to 100.[11]

2.3 Time Domain Stylized Facts

In this section we characterize the main features of the Italian business cycle by presenting time-domain summary statistics for the 1861-1995 period. We concentrate, for each detrended series, on measures of volatility (standard deviations), persistence (autocorrelations), and co-movements (cross-correlations) with the reference variable (GDP). In addition to the results for the whole sample, we present results for a breakdown of our sample into three sub-periods: pre-war (1861-1914), inter-war (1922-1939), and post-war (1951-1995). The 1915-1921 and 1940-1950 periods were excluded from the sample, due to the exceptional features of economic activity during and immediately after the two World Wars.[12]

In order to check for robustness, we will present results for both Hodrick-Prescott (HP) cyclical components and first differences of the series (in the following, tables indexed with *a* and *b* refer to HP-detrended and first differenced series, respectively). In the discussion of the results, however, we will focus mainly on HP-filtered data, while pointing out those findings which are

---

that the Hodrick-Prescott detrending procedure was made popular by empirical studies within the RBC framework.

[11]All variables were transformed into logarithms before detrending, with the exception of interest rates, inflation, and unemployment (for which absolute values were used), and net exports (which we expressed as a share of GDP).

[12]It would not be useful in this context to present rolling summary statistics (moving averages), as it is done in similar studies by Englund *et al.*, 1992; Hassler, since the behaviour of such statistics for Italian time series would be completely dominated by war-time years.

not robust to the detrending method, and providing an interpretation of the discrepancies where possible. We start by introducing the tables that present the results, and then discuss them by blocks of variables: GDP and expenditure components, monetary variables, and labour market variables. We then consider the main features of the Italian business cycle in relation to those of the other G7 countries and compare our results with those reported in earlier studies in the literature.

Tables 2.1a and 2.1b display volatility, persistence, and correlation statistics for annual long-run time series. The first panel refers to the whole sample period: the first two columns contain absolute and GDP-relative measures of amplitude (standard deviations), respectively; the third column shows, for each series, a measure of duration (the first order autocorrelation coefficient); the following five columns characterize cyclical co-movements by displaying correlation coefficients, up to two leads and lags, between each series and GDP.[13] The remaining three blocks in tables 2.1a and 2.1b show relative volatilities and correlation coefficients for each of the three sub-samples described above. Tables 2.2a and 2.2b present, in a similar way, summary statistics of GDP fluctuations in the G7 countries. In the discussion of the results we will follow Dolado *et al.* (1993) and Fiorito and Kollintzas (1994) in defining *a-cyclical* a variable whose contemporaneous correlation with GDP is less than 0.2 in absolute value; weakly *pro-cyclical* (*anti-cyclical*) if the correlation coefficient is between 0.2 and 0.5 (-0.2 and -0.5); and strongly *pro-cyclical* (*anti-cyclical*) if it is above (below) 0.5 (-0.5).

GDP and Expenditure Components

Consider first the volatility of GDP and its expenditure components, as measured by their absolute standard deviation. The volatility of GDP is highest in the inter-war period, and substantially lower in the post-war period. The standard-deviation of demand components also changed substantially over time: the inter-war period was much more volatile than the other two sub-periods and, with the exception of exports and consumption, the post-

[13] The lags for the correlation coefficients refer to GDP, so that if, for instance, the correlation is highest for lag -1 (+1), this should be interpreted as the given variable lagging (leading) the cycle by one year.

war period is somewhat less volatile than the pre-war period. With regard to relative volatilities, consumption is the only component displaying lower volatility than GDP. Investment, public expenditure, exports, and imports are substantially more volatile than output, with relative volatilities ranging from 2.5 to 5.6. The statistics by sub-period again reveal drastic changes in the relative volatility of GDP components over time. The relative volatilities of investment and public expenditure display a marked downward trend. The opposite holds for exports, while the relative volatility of exports was largely stable over time.

Autocorrelation coefficients, in the third column of tables 2.1a and 2.1b, indicate that public and private consumption display more regular and longer (lower frequency) fluctuations on average. Output fluctuations became progressively more persistent across the three sub-periods considered. This can be observed for growth rates in table 2.1b, while the extremely high inter-war coefficient for HP-detrended data (table 2.1b) is largely spurious, and does not reflect cyclical persistence.[14]

With regard to cyclical co-movements, as measured by cross-correlations with GDP, for the whole sample demand components are pro-cyclical and coincident with GDP, with the exceptions of public expenditure, which lags the cycle by one year, and exports, which lead the cycle by one year. This pattern of co-movements is virtually unchanged over time for consumption and investment (the only change is in the size of the correlation coefficients, which increases markedly for both variables), whereas it varies substantially in the three sub-periods for public expenditure and foreign trade variables. Interestingly, public expenditure is counter-cyclical and leading in the post-war period. Exports and imports are counter-cyclical and a-cyclical, respectively, in the pre-war period.

Monetary and Financial Variables

The absolute volatility of monetary and financial variables, similarly to GDP components, is highest in the inter-war period, and substantially lower in

[14]This is due to the fact that the HP-filter does not smooth out appropriately the wide swings corresponding to the two world wars, so that the features of the adjacent cycles are significantly affected. This point is discussed in more detail in section 2.4.

the post-war period. On the other hand, relative volatilities and the ranking among variables were virtually unchanged over time. Most variables have standard deviations between two and three times that of GDP. The duration is relatively high for most variables. Nominal interest rates have very low variability, whereas, due to the high volatility of inflation, real interest rates are almost twice as variable as real output.

Consider now the correlations between monetary variables and GDP. These are, in most cases, remarkably unstable over time. With the exception of price indices, most of the findings for the post-war period are reversed in the inter-war period. The nominal money stock (M2) is weakly counter-cyclical in the whole sample period. However, the counter-cyclical behaviour generally observed for nominal variables turns out to be due essentially to the deflation episodes of the inter-war period. M2 was indeed a-cyclical in the pre-war period and, interestingly, weakly pro-cyclical and leading in the post-war sub-period, respectively. Money velocity was pro-cyclical before the second World War, and counter-cyclical thereafter. In real terms, the money stock is pro-cyclical in the whole sample, although it is slightly counter-cyclical in the inter-war period. Money supply, both in real and nominal terms, leads the cycle by one year in the post-war period, while there is no clear pattern in the two earlier sub-periods.

Price variables are, for most of the sample, counter-cyclical. Both the GDP deflator and the wholesale price index are a-cyclical in the pre-war period, strongly counter-cyclical in the inter-war period, and weakly counter-cyclical in the post-war period. Quite remarkably, the inflation rate is consistently counter-cyclical throughout the sample. The real long-term interest rate is weakly pro-cyclical and coincident, whereas the nominal interest rate is a-cyclical throughout the sample. Both budget expenditures and revenues are highly volatile, pro-cyclical in the pre-war period, counter-cyclical between the world wars, and a-cyclical thereafter.

Labour Market Variables

The labour market variables in our data set display volatilities of the same order of magnitude as for GDP, with the exception of employment in the agriculture and service sectors, which are characterized by relatively less ample fluctuations. The total number of employees in the whole sample is less volatile than output, weakly pro-cyclical, and lags the cycle by one year. Employment fluctuations have become less volatile in the post-war period, as compared with the inter-war period. Looking at the disaggregation by sector, we observe that the sensitivity of employment to cyclical fluctuations is generally low. Manufacturing is the most cyclically-sensitive sector. Interestingly, services and agriculture display counter-cyclical behaviour in the pre- and post-war periods, respectively.

In the whole sample real wages are a-cyclical, with the only exception of the service sector, which displays weakly counter-cyclical behaviour. The a-cyclicality of real wages is essentially consistent throughout the sample in each sector, although manufacturing shows substantial changes between sub-periods. Labour productivity is strongly pro-cyclical and coincident. The Solow residual is weakly pro-cyclical, and leads the cycle by one year in the post-war period.

International comparison

Among the G7 economies, the Italian business cycle is characterized by a relatively high volatility coefficient over the entire sample. This result, however, is reversed in the decomposition into three sub-periods. As the latter exclude the world-war years, this finding indicates that the Italian economy was the most significantly affected, in an international comparison, by the fluctuations associated to the two world wars. Looking at absolute standard deviations, tables 2.2a and 2.2b also highlight that the temporal pattern of volatilities discussed above for the Italian economy is indeed common across countries: the volatility of GDP in the G7 economies is highest in the inter-war period, and substantially lower in the post-war period compared with both earlier periods (this pattern applies to both HP-detrended and first-differenced data).

Auto-correlation coefficients do not vary much across countries for the whole sample, as they lie between a minimum of 0.56 for Canada and a maximum of 0.74 for Germany. On the other hand there is wide variation in persistence over time: pre-war cycles display, for all countries but Germany, substantially higher frequency (lower duration). Consider next the degree of cyclical synchronization within the G7, as measured by the correlation coefficients between the GDP of each of the countries and Italy: in general the co-movements are relatively weak, with the only exception of the UK and, surprisingly, Japan. The degree of cyclical synchronization is highest in the inter-war period.

Comparative evidence

In the following paragraphs we compare the regularities identified for the Italian economy with the results obtained by other authors for different countries and sample periods. These sets of results are comparable as they all refer to cyclical components obtained with the HP filter. The only differences arise, apart from the definition of individual aggregates, by the fact that post-war studies generally use quarterly data, while long-run studies use annual data.

For post-war quarterly data, the main stylized facts found by Kydland and Prescott (1990) for the U.S., Blackburn and Ravn (1990) for the U.K., and Danthine and Girardine (1989) for a group of 11 industrialized countries, are the following: first, investment is more volatile than output, while consumption and employment are less volatile; second, all series display a high degree of serial correlation; third, all real variables and M2 are procyclical, while the GDP deflator is counter-cyclical; fourth, employment, exports, and investment lag the cycle, while the trade balance is a leading variable. The major differences in our findings for Italian post-war fluctuations are that consumption is more volatile than output, public expenditure is weakly counter-cyclical, and exports lead the cycle.

Using long-run annual data for the U.S. and the U.K., Correia *et al.* (1992) find results largely consistent with those for the post-war period, with some qualifications. For the U.S. economy, the serial correlation of most real variables is very low in the period 1889-1914, and remarkably high in the 1914-1950 period; consumption is more volatile than output before 1914; the relative volatility of government expenditure is extremely high when compared with the post-war period; prices are found to be procyclical in the 1889-1950 period. For the U.K., prices are a-cyclical, while, quite surprisingly, consumption, investment, and real wages are found to be counter-cyclical in the period 1914-1950. In our analysis, we find that serial correlations are very high in the interwar period, but this is interpreted as a spurious result due to the effects of HP-filtering on the entire sample. Real wages are a-cyclical throughout the sample in most sectors, although there are substantial changes between sub-periods in manufacturing, while labour productivity is strongly procyclical and coincident.[15]

In a comprehensive analysis of a data set for ten industrialized countries from 1860 to 1985, Backus and Kehoe (1992) identify the following regularities for GDP components: consumption is pro-cyclical and as volatile as output; investment is also pro-cyclical and two to four time more volatile than output; government expenditure is more volatile than output but has been counter-cyclical as often as pro-cyclical; net exports are counter-cyclical. Our findings largely confirm these results, with some additional qualifications: all GDP components are pro-cyclical and coincident, with the exception of public expenditure, lagging by one year, and exports, leading by one year. This pattern of co-movements is virtually unchanged over time for consumption and investment, whereas it varies substantially in the three sub-periods considered for public expenditure and trade variables. Public expenditure is counter-cyclical and leading in the post-war period, while exports and imports are counter-cyclical and a-cyclical, respectively, in the pre-war period.

Other major results in Backus and Kehoe (1992) are that GDP-correlations between countries are more pronounced in the post-war period than in the pre-war period; price changes have been more persistent in the post-war than in the pre-war period; prices are pro-cyclical in pre-war and inter-war periods while counter-cyclical in the post-war period in most of the ten countries considered; fluctuations of the money stock are less correlated with output in the post-war

[15]The main regularities identified by Englund *et al.* (1992) for Sweden, in the 1861-1988 period, can be summarised as follows: the variability of the series varies considerably over time, being highest in the inter-war period, while relative variabilities and comovements are fairly stable over time; GDP and consumption show the lowest standard deviation, whereas investment, exports, and imports have the highest volatility; GDP is contemporaneously uncorrelated with wages and productivity. In comparison, our results show substantial changes over time both in absolute and relative volatilities, as well as in the co-movements between variables.

period; inter-war fluctuations are uniformly larger than those of the post-war period. As for the degree of synchronization of output fluctuations, we find that this is highest in the inter-war period. Regarding the cyclical behaviour of prices, our results are quite striking, in that both the GDP deflator and the wholesale price index are a-cyclical in the pre-war period, strongly counter-cyclical in the inter-war period, and weakly counter-cyclical in the post-war period, while inflation is consistently counter-cyclical throughout the sample.

2.4 The Post-War Stabilization of Aggregate Fluctuations

The post-war stabilization of macroeconomic fluctuations is a debated empirical issue. The evidence on the possible dampening of business cycles can in fact be relevant both for evaluating the efficacy of stabilization policies and for discriminating between alternative economic theories. As for the policy debate, many authors have interpreted the dampening of economic fluctuations as the result of counter-cyclical stabilization policies and the more widespread role of automatic stabilizers (see e.g. Baily, 1978, and Zarnowitz and Moore, 1986). If this interpretation is correct, a better understanding of the evidence could provide useful policy recommendations. As for the theoretical debate, the evidence of reduced amplitude of economic fluctuations, coupled with a reduction in the flexibility of prices and wages, would cast doubts on many traditional explanations of business cycles and open the way to alternative interpretations (Taylor, 1986; DeLong and Summers, 1986).

Until the mid-eighties, the consensus among economists was, essentially on the basis of the evidence for the U.S. economy, that the amplitude of macroeconomic fluctuations had decreased significantly after World War II.[16] This commonly held view was challenged by Romer (1986, 1989), who argued that the apparent decrease in the severity of economic fluctuations was due essentially to the inconsistency of data construction techniques over different time periods. A different kind of critique to the consensus view came from

[16] See e.g. Lucas (1977), p. 218: "[...] Too striking a phenomenon [...] is the general reduction in amplitude of all series in the 25 years following World War II".

Sheffrin (1988), who extended the empirical analysis of post-war stabilization to six European countries, and found no significant evidence of reduction in the severity of business cycles.

As a result, a number of studies have recently reconsidered the issue of postwar stabilization, extending the analysis in different directions. On the one hand, some researchers have approached the question of stabilization in terms of the relative duration, rather than the relative volatility, of pre-war and post-war business cycles.[17] On the other hand, many studies have maintained the focus on business cycle amplitude, while extending the analysis to a larger number of countries.[18]

For the Italian economy, Sheffrin (1988) found the reduction of the volatility of GDP growth rates to be statistically non-significant, while Backus and Kehoe (1992) found a substantial reduction in the volatility of Hodrick-Prescott detrended GDP. Ardeni and Gallegati (1994) found evidence of a substantial reduction in the volatility of the short-run fluctuations of real GDP. Their results, however, are difficult to interpret due to the inclusion of the world-war periods in the sample. Schlitzer (1995), on the basis of a different data set (Rossi *et al.*, 1993), obtained mixed results which highlighted the sensitivity to the choice of the detrending technique. Gallegati and Gallegati (1995) analyzed a set of physical production series, to overcome the difficulties associated with deflating aggregate nominal series, finding evidence of relatively small changes of volatility over time at disaggregate level.

Overall, the evidence presented in the literature for the Italian economy is not conclusive and difficult to interpret, due to substantial differences in the choice of data sets, sample periods, and empirical techniques. Against this background, this section investigates the stabilization of economic fluctuations for the Italian economy, comparing the results obtained with alternative

[17]Diebold and Rudebusch (1990, 1992) applied non-parametric tests to cyclical phase durations, finding strong evidence of a postwar shift toward longer expansions and shorter contractions, although no evidence for a shift in whole-cycle durations. Watson (1994) found evidence of duration stabilization, but attributed it to differences in the way that prewar and postwar reference dates were chosen by the NBER.

[18]In particular, Backus and Kehoe (1992) found pre-war fluctuations generally larger than those of the post-war period, although with substantial differences across countries.

data sources, detrending techniques, and sample periods[19], and examining the evidence on the structural changes driving the aggregate results.

Table 2.3 reports standard deviations, by sub-period and by data source, for both first differenced and Hodrick-Prescott filtered GDP. Regardless of the source of the data, the volatility of growth rates is substantially lower in the post-war period compared to the previous two periods.[20] Looking at HP filtered data, the volatility of fluctuations was relatively low and on a rising trend from 1861 to 1914, very high between the two world wars, and relatively low in the post-war period. Interestingly, the difference between the pre-WWI and the post-WWII periods is relatively small.

What explains the differences between the results obtained with the two detrending procedures? Figures 2.1 and 2.2 provide a simple answer to this question by displaying, together with the full-sample series, first-difference and HP-filtered cyclical components for each of the sub-periods considered. A comparison of the two figures shows that the problem lies in the fact that the HP-filter does not smooth out appropriately the wide swings corresponding to the two world wars. This implies that the features of the adjacent cycles included in the sub-samples are significantly affected, as it is shown in the bottom part of figure 2.2. This figure shows, in particular, how the volatility of fluctuations in the inter-war and post-war periods is artificially increased. This explains why both Backus and Kehoe (1992), using ISTAT data, and Schlitzer (1995)[21], using Rossi *et al.* (1993) data, find little evidence of a decrease in the volatility of fluctuations between the pre-war and the post-war periods: their results are spurious, in the sense that they are determined by inappropriate detrending.

[19] In order to maintain the comparability with previous studies and check the robustness of the results to the use of alternative sources and methods of construction of series, we also present results obtained with each of the data sets described above. We will thus refer to the following five data sets: ISTAT, Fuà, Maddison, Rossi, and FG. See Stanca (1998) for details.

[20] It is interesting to note that in some cases the volatility of the three-period sub-samples is higher than the volatility of the corresponding five-period sub-samples. This reflects the fact that, although stationary, GDP growth rates still have much of their variability at low frequencies.

[21] This also explains why the tests presented by Schlitzer (1995) are significant for first differences and more flexible (higher lambda coefficient) HP filters.

Table 2.4 presents test statistics of the null hypothesis of constant standard deviations across different sub-samples. The upper part of the table, based on GDP growth rates, confirms the previous qualitative indications: the decrease in post-WWII volatility with respect to both the pre-WWI and the inter-war periods (and to a combination of the two) is statistically significant. Note also that the tests fail to reject the hypothesis of constant volatility before and after WWI. The bottom part of table 2.4 shows that, by using the HP detrending procedure, there is little evidence of significantly different volatilities between the pre-war and the post-war periods. As explained above, this conclusion, which is analogous to some of the findings in the literature, is unwarranted, and can be attributed to the artificially high GDP volatility produced by HP detrending in the post-war period.

A number of different interpretations have been proposed in the literature for the reduced volatility of economic activity between the pre-war and the post-war periods (see e.g. Zarnowitz, 1992).[22] We now focus on the extent to which the decline in output volatility can be attributed to structural changes in the composition of output. Figures 2.3 and 2.4 plot the decomposition of GDP into the shares of its main components, with respect to both the formation of resources and their use. As for resource formation, the share of agriculture declines progressively throughout the period, mirrored by the steady growth of the service sector. The share of the industrial sector grows substantially in the two decades after World War II, but it stabilizes thereafter. As for the use of resources, the overall pattern is less clear-cut. The share of fixed investment has increased steadily over the sample, whereas the share of private consumption is lower in the postwar period (although on an increasing trend).

How does the composition of GDP relate to its overall variability? We should consider both the role of the changing composition of GDP, for given relative levels of components' volatility, and the role of changes over time of the volatility of individual components, for a given composition. Table 2.5 shows, by component and by sub-period, volatilities (relative to GDP) of in-

[22] Zarnowitz (1992) identifies eight main explanations: structural changes in the private economy; increases in the size of government; institutional changes; stabilization poliicies; gains in learning and conficence; smaller shocks to the economy; gains in technology, information, and knowledge; changes in the flexibility of wages and prices.

dividual components by formation and use of resources, respectively. Looking at the decomposition by sector of formation, even though the magnitude in the volatility of the GDP components is very different across sub-periods, the ranking is unchanged over time. The relative volatility of agriculture is, consistently over the whole sample, about twice as large as that of the manufacturing and service sectors. Thus the decline in the overall variability of GDP reflects in part the progressive increase in the shares of the secondary and tertiary sectors, which by the end of the sample account for about 90 per cent of GDP. On the other hand, it should be noted that the volatility of individual supply components does not display any trend, although the inter-war period is characterized by much higher volatility then the other two sub-periods. Such a pattern of progressive decrease in relative volatility is instead evident in the decomposition by use of resources. The relative volatilities of public consumption and, significantly, fixed capital formation and inventories (the two most volatile components) display an overall decreasing trend. Private consumption, on the other hand, is characterized by progressively increasing volatility. The composition of GDP by use, as noted above, does not show any systematic pattern, if not for the decrease in the share of private consumption and the increase in the share of fixed capital formation after WWII.

Overall the figures indicate that the decrease in the variability of GDP reflects on the one hand a re-composition towards more stable components on the supply side, while on the other hand a progressive reduction in the amplitude of the most volatile components, against a roughly constant composition, on the demand side.

2.5 Classical Analysis: Individual Cycles

This section departs from the *representative cycle* assumption, and provides a description of the main features of Italian aggregate fluctuations taking individual cycles and phases as separate entities, as in the classical NBER method of analysis. We start by identifying a business cycle chronology for the Italian economy and then present the main regularities for individual cycles and phases. The next section provides a brief historical account of the main factors and features of each cyclical episode.

For the identification of the business cycle chronologies we developed a turning point identification procedure (TP5). This GAUSS procedure provides a simplified version of the original NBER procedure developed by Bry and Boschan (1971). Its main advantage is that it does not require any ex-post judgemental interventions for the identification of turning points. In addition, TP5 incorporates explicit criteria for the duration and amplitude of cycles, and can be used for the analysis of both classical and growth cycles.

A business cycle chronology for the Italian economy was obtained by comparing the turning points identified for GDP from two sources. The first series is from Rossi *et al.* (1993) for the 1891-1992 period, and from Fuà for the 1861-1890 period. The second GDP series is the chain index proposed in Fuà and Gallegati (1996). As discussed in section 2.2, the FG chain index aims at solving, at least partially, the difficulties arising from expressing long-run time series at constant prices of years which are far apart in the sample period, by using a system of values prevailing at times closer to the dates to be compared. The cyclical components of the two series, and the turning points identified with the TP5 procedure, are shown in figure 2.5. The corresponding cyclical chronologies, and the corresponding summary statistics, are displayed in tables 2.6 and 2.7.

The comparison of the chronologies obtained with the two GDP series reveals an almost complete correspondence for the post-war period, but substantial differences for the earlier periods. In particular, the cyclical component of the Rossi *et al.* (1993) series does not display major fluctuations during the 1920s (thus missing the 1920-22 and 1925-27 contractions which are quite evident in the chain index series), while it emphasizes cyclical movements just before the turn of the century, indicating two extra cycles during the 1890s with respect to the chain index. In the three decades after unity, the reconstructions based on Fuà (1981) do not show marked cyclical behaviour during the 1870s. On the whole, it appears that, in order to establish a cyclical chronology, the chain index not only is more appropriate from a statistical point of view, but also provides turning point dates which are more consistent with the historical features of individual cyclical episodes (as described in the next section).

We thus propose the following business cycle chronology. For the pre-war period the trough-years are: 1863, 1867, 1872, 1881, 1889, 1897, 1906, 1910; while the peak-years are: 1866, 1870, 1875, 1886, 1891, 1901, 1907, 1916. For the inter-war period the trough-years are: 1919, 1922, 1927, 1934, 1945; while the peak-years are 1916, 1920, 1925, 1929, 1940. For the post-war period the trough-years are: 1945, 1958, 1965, 1972, 1975, 1983, 1993; while the peak-years are 1951, 1962, 1970, 1974, 1980, 1990.

Looking at the summary statistics for the whole sample (tables 2.6 and 2.7), growth cycles have an average duration slightly above seven years, and an average amplitude of about 20 percentage points (the chain index displays somewhat wider fluctuations). Excluding the two world-wars from the sample, cycles are on average shorter (6.2 years) and substantially less pronounced (the amplitude falls to about 14 per cent). There seem to be relatively large asymmetries between expansions and contractions in terms of both duration and amplitude. In particular, there is evidence of steepness asymmetry , in that expansions are on average longer than contractions: 4.6 and 2.5 years, respectively, for the Rossi-Fuà series and 3.8 and 3.3 years, respectively, for the FG series.

These average statistics do not reflect the substantial heterogeneity existing among individual cycles and phases. The duration of full cycles for the chain index ranges from 3 to 13 years. The duration of both expansions and contractions ranges from a minimum of 1 year to a maximum of 7 years. The heterogeneity is even more pronounced in terms of amplitude. Even omitting the cycles associated to world wars, which inflate substantially the average statistics, full cycle amplitude varies from about 7 to above 20 percentage points. Looking at sub-periods separately, fluctuations are shortest and most pronounced between the wars, while relatively long and dampened in the post-war period. Partially due to the exclusion of some minor cycles, pre-war fluctuations display on average relatively large duration and amplitude.

Considering next the co-movements between variables, the main features are considered in table 2.8, which displays, for selected variables, phase-specific changes (relative to trend) and cycle-specific correlations with GDP. The main results can be summarized as follows. First, the sign and size of cycle-specific correlations with GDP of main aggregate variables vary widely across individual cyclical episodes (although the procyclical behaviour of consumption and investment is quite consistent across cycles). It should be noted that such cyclical heterogeneity cannot be accounted for solely by breaking down the full sample into three sub-samples. Second, the behaviour of each series also varies substantially across individual cyclical phases. Finally, expansions and contractions do not display a symmetric behaviour in terms of co-movements.

2.6 Individual Cycles: Facts and Factors

This section considers the factors and features which characterize each of the cyclical episodes identified in the previous paragraphs. We follow Fuà (1981) in adopting the following periodization: the Pre-war period, divided into the *post-unity* (1861-1896) and *Giolitti* (1897-1913) periods; the Inter-war (or *Fascist*) period, between 1921 and 1938; and the Post-war period, further divided into the *economic miracle* years (1950-1973) and the *post-oil-shock* years (1974-1995).

The *post-unity* period, between 1861 and 1897, was characterized by sharp and relatively severe output fluctuations, against a background of very low average growth.[23] In evaluating the cyclical behaviour of the Italian economy in its early years, it is important to consider its essentially agricultural base: agriculture accounted for about 46 per cent of real GDP in 1861 and 37.6 per cent in 1913 (Fuà, 1981). This helps to explain the irregular character and the relatively high number and short duration of cyclical episodes in the pre-war period.

The economy expanded steadily in the initial years after unity (with the exception of 1863), fuelled by a number of good harvests and the broadening of the internal market, to reach a peak in 1866, more than 6 percentage points above trend. A sharp contraction (11 per cent), however, hit the economy in 1867, due to a number of coincident factors: the consequences of heavy military defeats in the Prussian war against Austria, a particularly bad agricultural

[23]The Italian take-off is generally recognised to have started only after 1896 (see e.g. Fuà, 1981; Toniolo, 1978), relatively late in the European context.

harvest, and the drop in manufacturing output which followed the introduction of the *corso forzoso* in 1866 (see Toniolo, 1978, p. 8). The ensuing gradual recovery was interrupted by a minor contraction (3.4 per cent of amplitude from peak to trough) between 1870 and 1872, to resume its course until the 1875 peak. The second half of the 1870s witnessed a prolonged contraction until 1881, interrupted only by a minor recovery between 1878 and 1880. The downturn was exacerbated by the onset of the international depression which lasted from the early 1870s to the mid-1880s, when falling prices reflected excess productive capacity combined with slowly growing markets in most industrialised countries.

In the early 1880s the economy went through a gradual recovery, with the cyclical component of GDP increasing by about 7 per cent between 1881 and 1886. The end of the expansion is generally attributed to the impact of the increase in tariffs in 1887 (which followed some earlier mild increases in 1878). The *tariff war* which followed between 1888 and 1898, in particular between France and Italy, had extremely negative effects on agricultural exports. The short recovery between 1889 and 1891 was followed by the most severe and protracted recession of the pre-war period, as output fell to 7 per cent below trend at the trough in 1897. The effects of this contraction were amplified by a widespread financial crisis, as the tariff war reduced credit activities of the major banks, which were heavily dependent on agriculture. This, in turn, had damaging effects on industrial expansion, while the international economic situation also worsened during this period, leading to a substantial withdrawal of foreign capital.

The deep crisis of the first half of the 1890s set the ground for the *Giolitti* period, between 1897 and 1913, acknowledged by most observers as the Italian take-off period, and characterized by very rapid industrial growth. The favourable developments were supported by rapidly growing markets abroad, as the great world depression and the tariff war came to an end at the turn of the century, and internally by the development of a German-type banking system during the early 1890s. The industrial expansion, however, slowed down temporarily as a result of the 1907 international crisis.

In the years between the two world-wars, the Italian economy experienced severe cyclical fluctuations. Although the first world war inflicted substantial costs on Italy, the industrial sector benefited initially from the rapid growth in demand and high profits. Together with the dramatic increase in public expenditure, this helped the economy to enter the ensuing contractionary phase only after 1916.[24] By 1919 the cyclical component of output had dropped by 16 percentage points, more than 6 per cent below trend.

The recovery that followed was short-lived, as the economic situation worsened even further, due, among other factors, to a particularly bad harvest in 1920, and mounting pressures on the banking system in 1921.[25] The post-war crisis was particularly acute, and the economy reached its lowest level below trend for the inter-war period at the cyclical trough in 1922. Unemployment was high, inflation soared (the cyclical component of the GDP deflator increased by 20 per cent between 1920 and the 1922 trough), and strike activity was widespread.

Following the formation of the first Fascist government in late 1922, and until 1925, the economy underwent a rapid recovery. This upswing was supported by subdued wage growth, which boosted profits and in turn investment, and a competitive devaluation of the exchange rate, which stimulated Italian exports. Investment and exports increased by about 30 per cent during the expansion, whereas consumption was virtually unchanged and public expenditure, reflecting the government's efforts to balance the budget, decreased substantially (see table 2.8).

The second half of the 1920s, however, brought the expansion to an end, due on one hand to the introduction of the first Fascist autarchic policies (the *Battle for Grain* was announced in 1925 and, in an attempt to create a strong currency, the lira was upvalued in 1926), and on the other to the beginning of the world great depression. The economy experienced a short contraction between 1925 and 1927, followed by a brief recovery which came to an abrupt end with the stock market crash of 1929 and the beginning of the world-wide depression, whose effects lasted in Italy throughout 1934. The following

[24]It should be noted that, on the basis of the Fuà series, 1918 is identified as the peak-year (see e.g. Toniolo, 1978).

[25]This was due to failure of large firms such as Ilva and Ansaldo, which led to the collapse of Banco di Roma and Banca Italiana di Sconto (see Zamagni, 1993, and Toniolo, 1988).

years, until the beginning of the war, saw a gradual recovery, supported by the devaluation of the lira in 1936, as the strong-lira policy was abandoned, and the rise in public expenditure due to the preparation of the Abissinia war starting in 1935. The gains secured by the ascending cyclical phase in the second half of the 1930s, however, were swept away by the destruction of capital equipment and infrastructure brought about by world war II. By 1945 real output had dropped by more than 40 per cent relative to the beginning of the recession in 1940.[26]

The *economic miracle* years were marked by rapid and stable growth with cyclical fluctuations of minor significance.[27] A number of factors, however, hampered the recovery in the immediate post-war period. Raw materials were in short supply, lack of foreign currency restrained imports, agriculture was hit further by bad weather in 1947, while war-time inflation intensified throughout 1947, to be brought under control only in 1948. In spite of these negative conditions, the economy had regained its pre-war strength by 1950. Such a rapid recovery was made possible by substantial aid from the Allies, starting in 1943, in the form of grants, loans at favourable rates and, initially, foodstuffs and materials.

The early 1950s saw the consolidation of the recovery from the war-time depression. The economy benefited from a long period of stable and rapid growth (the *economic miracle* years), interrupted only temporarily by a minor downturn in 1958, and reaching a peak in 1962. Due to increases in wages and prices, and the resulting loss in competitiveness, the Italian economy ran into a deep balance of payment crisis in 1963. As a consequence, monetary and credit restrictions were introduced in an attempt to deflate the economy, which negatively affected industrial investment.

The economy recovered slowly from the 1963 crisis, as the effects of the associated restrictive policies protracted until the 1965 trough. The following expansion, although particularly strong in 1966 and 1967, was dampened

[26] In addition, inflation increased dramatically, fuelled by widespread hoarding and speculation, high government expenditure, and the Allied injection of money.

[27] These were indeed the years when it became a common view among economists that the business cycle was *obsolete* (see the much-quoted collection of papers in Bronfenbrenner, 1969). As fluctuations became worldwide shorter and more damped, the attention shifted towards the determinants of long-run growth.

thereafter by the repercussions of the widespread social unrest in 1969 (the so called *hot autumn*). Due to the acute tensions in the labour market, the 1970-72 contraction was characterized, as in the 1962-65 episode, by an increase in inflation and balance of payments difficulties.

The following recovery was interrupted by the 1973 oil crisis. Italy entered the associated contractionary phase, however, one year later than the other G7 countries (this was the only post-war contraction, together with the 1992-93 recession, when real output decreased in absolute terms). While the economy underwent a gradual recovery in the second half of the 1970s, this was interrupted by the second oil shock in 1979. Italian GDP started to pick up only in 1983, relatively late in international comparison. Output continued to expand steadily throughout 1990, resulting in the longest expansionary phase to date. Following the 1993 trough, the economy has grown strongly, led by an upturn in domestic demand and by the rise in exports, in turn spurred by the progressive depreciation of the lira after the September 1992 currency crisis.

2.7 Are Business Cycles All Alike?

The analysis in the preceding section highlighted substantial heterogeneity, for both cycles and phases, in terms of duration, amplitude, and co-movements between variables. In this section we extend the analysis to a sample of ten industrialized countries and provide formal tests of the hypothesis, implicit in most of the recent empirical literature, that business cycles are all alike (see Stanca, 1999b). More precisely, we consider the evidence on the stability of the propagation mechanism over time. Our testing procedure is similar to the approach of Blanchard and Watson (1986), who investigated US post-war quarterly time series.[28] We also consider the evidence on steepness asymmetry, that is on whether cyclical phases are symmetric in terms of duration (see Neftci, 1984; DeLong and Summers, 1986; Sichel, 1993).

Our results are derived in three steps. The first step is to calculate mea-

[28]Blanchard and Watson (1986) concentrate on cyclical correlations, finding that, although correlations are very different across cycles, such differences are not statistically significant.

sures of amplitude, duration, and co-movements for individual cycles in the ten countries of our data set.[29] For each country we identify a business cycle chronology by applying the TP5 procedure to the detrended real GDP series, and divide the sample accordingly into cyclical sub-samples. We then calculate amplitude and duration statistics for both cycles and phases, and cross-correlations between each variable and GDP for each cyclical episode. The corresponding cross-cycle average statistics are presented in table 2.9, with duration and amplitude reported in years and percentage points, respectively. Overall, the cross-cycle average statistics match closely the features highlighted in the time domain summary statistics presented by Backus and Kehoe (1992).

The second step is to consider the representativeness of the average cyclical statistics. This is examined in table 2.10, which presents the cross-cycle standard deviations of cyclical correlations, amplitudes and durations. The degree of heterogeneity is, for most countries, remarkably high. In particular, the cross-cycle variability of cyclical correlations appears striking. In addition to measures of variability, the last column displays the average difference in duration between expansions and contractions. These statistics suggest, at a qualitative level, the presence of steepness asymmetry. Taken together, these results provide a qualitative indication that, in our sample of ten industrialized countries, business cycles are not all alike over time, and that recessions are not mirror images of expansions.

The third step is to evaluate the statistical significance of the observed cross-cycle variability and cyclical asymmetry. More precisely, the question we pose is how likely are, under the null hypothesis of a stable propagation mechanism: a) the observed variability in cyclical correlation coefficients, durations, and amplitudes; and b) the differences in the duration of expansion and contractions. To answer this question we derived an empirical distribution of the cross-cycle standard deviation of durations, amplitudes, and

[29]The time series analysed in this section are based on an updated and revised version of the Backus and Kehoe (1992) long run international data set (see section 2.2). The data set consists of annual observations between 1860 and 1996 for real GDP (Y), Investment (I), Private Consumption (C), Public Consumption (G), Net exports (NX), Money stock (M), and the GDP deflator (P) for 10 industrialized countries (Australia, Canada, Denmark, Germany, Italy, Japan, Norway, Sweden, United Kingdom, United States).

cyclical correlation coefficients, and of the average difference in the duration of expansions and contractions.

The empirical distribution was obtained by simulation as follows. Consider first the cyclical correlations. We estimated a bivariate VAR for GDP and each of the variables under consideration, determining the lag-length by sequential testing. The bivariate process was then simulated by bootstrapping, using disturbances drawn with replacement from the estimated residuals (similar results were obtained with a more restrictive Monte Carlo simulation, where the disturbances for the simulations were drawn from a normal distribution with standard deviation equal to that of the estimated residuals). We thus generated 1000 simulated samples of 132 observations, which we used to identify turning points, and the corresponding cyclical subsamples, by applying the TP5 turning point procedure described above. We then computed, for each simulated series, cycle-specific correlations and the corresponding standard deviations (across cyclical subsamples), thus obtaining an empirical distribution for such cross-cycle standard deviations. The procedure for the univariate statistics was similar, except that univariate autoregressive models were estimated and simulated (with the lag-length being determined by a combination of the Akaike and Schwarz information criteria).

Having obtained an empirical distribution, we calculated the corresponding p-values for the statistics of interest calculated from the actual data. These figures, reported in table 2.11, are the probabilities that, in the corresponding empirical distributions, the statistics of interest (the standard deviation of cyclical correlations, for instance) exceed the values obtained in the actual sample. Small values thus indicate that the statistics observed in the actual data are surprisingly large under the representative cycle null hypothesis.

A number of results emerge from table 2.11. First, under the representative cycle null hypothesis of stable linear propagation mechanism, the variability in the amplitude and duration of individual cycles and phases is surprisingly large for most variables (columns 1 and 2). That is, we would reject, for almost all variables considered, the hypothesis that business cycles are all alike, formulated in the sense that the variation in cyclical duration and amplitude is statistically negligible. Second, and more important, the observed cyclical heterogeneity is generally statistically significant also for co-movements between variables, although this result is somewhat less general: correlations are very different across cycles for most variables, and such variability is statistically significant for about half of the variables considered (columns 3 to 9). Third, as shown in the last column, the evidence of steepness asymmetry (different duration between expansions and contractions) is also generally statistically significant.

2.8 Summary and Conclusions

This chapter has analysed the main features of business cycles in Italy in historical perspective. Our motivation was, on the one hand, to define what facts should be explained and replicated by theoretical models, and, on the other hand, to assess to what extent business cycles are all alike over time.

In the first part of the chapter, we presented the results of a time-domain descriptive analysis of Italian business cycles in the 1861-1995 period, and provided a small set of robust time-domain regularities. The main findings can be summarized as follows:

1. Over the whole sample, GDP components are procyclical and coincident, with the exception of public expenditure, lagging by one year, and exports, leading by one year. This pattern of co-movements is virtually unchanged over time for consumption and investment, whereas it varies substantially in the three sub-periods for public expenditure and trade variables. Public expenditure is counter-cyclical and leading in the post-war period, while exports and imports are counter-cyclical and a-cyclical, respectively, in the pre-war period.

2. There are substantial changes over time both in absolute and relative volatilities. Consumption is the only aggregate demand component displaying lower volatility than GDP. Other demand components are, consistently over time, substantially more volatile than output, with relative volatilities ranging from 2 to 6 times that of GDP.

3. Both the GDP deflator and the wholesale price index are a-cyclical in

the pre-war period, strongly counter-cyclical in the inter-war period, and weakly counter-cyclical in the post-war period, while inflation is consistently counter-cyclical throughout the sample. Real wages are a-cyclical throughout the sample in most sectors, although there are substantial changes between sub-periods in manufacturing, and labour productivity is strongly procyclical and coincident. In real terms, the money stock is procyclical in the whole sample, although it is slightly counter-cyclical in the inter-war period. Money supply, both in real and nominal terms, leads the cycle by one year in the post-war period, while there is no clear pattern in the two earlier sub-periods.

4. Among the G7 countries, the Italian business cycle is characterized by a relatively high volatility coefficient over the entire sample. This result, however, is reversed in the decomposition into three sub-periods, as the Italian economy was the most significantly affected by the fluctuations associated to the two world wars. The volatility of GDP in the G7 economies is highest in the inter-war period, and substantially lower in the post-war period compared to both earlier periods. The degree of international synchronization of output fluctuations is highest in the inter-war period.

We also examined the evidence on the post-war stabilization of fluctuations. We found robust evidence that the amplitude of GDP fluctuations has decreased significantly in the post-war period. The decrease in the variability of GDP was shown to reflect a re-composition towards more stable components on the supply side, and a progressive reduction in the amplitude of the most volatile components, against a roughly constant composition, on the demand side.

In the second part of the chapter, we removed the restrictive *representative cycle* assumption, and provided a description of the main features of Italian aggregate fluctuations taking individual cycles and cyclical phases as separate entities, as in the NBER tradition. Our main findings can be summarized as follows:

1. Over the whole sample period, growth cycles have an average duration

slightly above 7 years, and an average amplitude of about 20 percentage points. Excluding from the sample the two World-War cycles are on average shorter (6.2 years) and substantially less pronounced (the amplitude falls to 14 per cent). There are relatively large asymmetries between expansions and contractions in terms of both duration and amplitude. In particular, there is evidence of steepness asymmetry, in that expansions are on average longer than contractions, and of deepness asymmetry, in that contractions are deeper than expansions.

2. The duration of full cycles ranges from 3 to 13 years, and the duration of both expansions and contractions ranges from a minimum of 1 year to a maximum of 7 years. Even omitting the cycles associated with the world wars, full cycle amplitude varies from about 7 to above 20 percentage points. Fluctuations are shortest and most pronounced between the wars, while relatively long and dampened in the post-war period. Partially due to the exclusion of some minor cycles, pre-war fluctuations display on average relatively large duration and amplitude.

3. With regard to cyclical co-movements, the sign and size of cycle-specific correlations with GDP of main aggregate variables varies widely across individual cyclical episodes, although among GDP components, the procyclical behaviour of consumption and investment is quite consistent across cycles. There are substantial differences across individual cyclical phases and, in addition, expansions and contractions do not display a symmetric behaviour in terms of co-movements between variables.

Finally, we presented the results of formal tests of various aspects of the *representative cycle* hypothesis. We found that the heterogeneity of specific cycles and phases, in terms of duration, amplitude, and co-movements between variables, is in most cases statistically significant. Overall, our conclusion is that business cycles are not at all alike, and neither are cyclical phases. That is, the univariate features of economic time series and, more importantly, the co-movements among the main economic aggregates, are not qualitatively similar across different cyclical episodes.

These results have implications for both econometric practice and economic theory. First, at the empirical level, our findings suggest that, in order to improve our understanding of economic fluctuations, descriptive analyses should not restrict the attention to sample second moments, but also study the features of individual cycles and phases. Second, at the theoretical level, the rejection of the representative cycle hypothesis underlines the difficulties of developing theories providing a unified explanation of *the* business cycle, while suggesting a research strategy focusing on the interactions between agents' distribution dynamics at the micro level and aggregate fluctuations. This approach will be followed in chapters 4 and 5.

Table 2.1a: Time domain summary statistics (1861-1995): HP

	Whole sample (1861-1995)								Pre-war					Inter-war					Post-war				
	St.Dev.		Aut.	Correlation with GDP					S.D.	Aut.	Corr. with GDP			S.D.	Aut.	Corr. with GDP			S.D.	Aut.	Corr. with GDP		
	Abs.	Rel.	-1	-2	-1	0	1	2	Rel.	-1	-1	0	1	Rel.	-1	-1	0	1	Rel.	-1	-1	0	1
GDP and expenditure components																							
GDP	5.01	1.00	0.52	0.10	0.52	1.00	0.52	0.10	2.66	-0.09	-0.09	1.00	-0.09	4.89	0.73	0.73	1.00	0.73	3.17	0.54	0.61	1.00	0.54
Private Consumption	3.58	0.71	0.64	-0.10	0.33	0.66	0.52	0.35	0.63	0.38	0.01	0.40	0.05	0.60	0.48	0.69	0.73	0.34	0.62	0.65	0.58	0.76	0.37
Investment	18.11	3.61	0.38	-0.20	-0.08	0.29	0.25	0.15	6.70	0.02	-0.35	0.29	-0.09	2.97	0.71	0.47	0.51	0.36	1.46	0.60	0.66	0.82	0.33
Public Consumption	19.45	3.88	0.75	0.34	0.42	0.40	0.12	-0.16	5.14	0.74	0.32	0.43	0.15	2.79	0.65	0.13	0.20	0.25	1.19	0.79	-0.02	-0.13	-0.19
Exports	27.90	5.57	0.46	-0.15	0.16	0.56	0.44	0.16	3.02	0.20	-0.12	-0.32	-0.11	3.83	0.52	0.64	0.53	0.30	2.66	0.77	0.18	0.44	0.55
Imports	12.74	2.54	0.33	-0.20	0.14	0.39	0.45	0.19	3.24	0.27	0.08	0.02	0.32	3.81	0.21	0.60	0.37	0.18	1.95	0.49	0.34	0.70	0.41
Net Exports	0.78	0.16	0.34	0.01	-0.02	0.02	-0.04	0.06	0.23	0.39	-0.15	-0.07	-0.35	0.17	0.25	-0.43	0.10	0.16	0.28	0.38	-0.29	-0.42	0.05
Monetary variables																							
Money stock (M2)	9.24	1.84	0.83	-0.13	-0.18	-0.28	-0.32	-0.24	2.33	0.65	0.34	0.08	-0.13	2.34	0.79	-0.58	-0.82	-0.77	1.81	0.85	0.04	0.21	0.34
GDP deflator	15.07	3.01	0.84	-0.50	-0.53	-0.40	-0.13	0.09	2.38	0.53	0.12	-0.03	0.03	2.66	0.86	-0.50	-0.66	-0.57	2.01	0.88	-0.15	-0.13	-0.16
Money velocity	9.47	1.89	0.58	-0.63	-0.39	0.16	0.38	0.43	1.94	0.17	-0.29	0.35	0.17	1.80	0.51	0.36	0.64	0.47	1.13	0.44	-0.03	-0.07	-0.55
Inflation rate	8.48	1.69	0.50	0.05	-0.23	-0.47	-0.40	-0.14	2.06	0.13	0.10	-0.05	-0.02	1.75	-0.02	0.02	-0.32	-0.33	1.20	0.73	0.04	-0.14	-0.54
Wholesale price index	18.94	3.78	0.79	-0.38	-0.42	-0.41	-0.24	0.07	3.14	0.73	0.23	0.18	0.15	2.74	0.76	-0.37	-0.54	-0.48	2.23	0.75	-0.22	-0.19	-0.37
Real interest rate	8.47	1.69	0.50	-0.03	0.24	0.47	0.38	0.11	2.05	0.12	-0.09	0.06	0.01	1.77	0.00	-0.02	0.30	0.29	1.16	0.75	0.11	0.12	0.40
Nominal interest rate	0.95	0.19	0.63	0.14	0.13	0.02	-0.18	-0.25	0.17	0.67	0.23	0.12	-0.11	0.11	0.49	-0.03	-0.18	-0.44	0.47	0.67	0.29	-0.04	-0.41
Nominal GDP	13.83	2.76	0.81	-0.51	-0.38	-0.07	0.05	0.14	2.50	0.52	0.09	0.35	0.03	2.13	0.77	-0.26	-0.36	-0.36	2.02	0.85	0.02	0.15	-0.01
Real money stock	9.96	1.99	0.66	0.64	0.63	0.34	-0.10	-0.36	1.84	0.24	0.27	0.14	-0.18	1.40	0.44	0.03	-0.10	-0.17	1.29	0.65	0.26	0.50	0.71
Budget expenditures	15.36	3.07	0.72	-0.04	0.04	0.15	0.14	0.08	4.82	0.70	0.32	0.37	0.09	3.36	0.68	-0.46	-0.56	-0.38	2.88	0.60	0.02	0.06	0.04
Budget revenues	15.68	3.13	0.78	-0.45	-0.26	0.12	0.35	0.28	2.20	0.56	0.26	0.27	0.20	2.29	0.69	-0.53	-0.35	-0.02	3.31	0.84	0.02	0.19	0.24
Labour market variables																							
Employment - Total	1.81	0.36	0.75	0.23	0.24	0.12	-0.06	-0.16	.	.	.	.	.	0.64	0.78	0.48	0.32	0.20	0.31	0.65	0.21	0.19	-0.18
Employment - Agr.	1.35	0.27	0.35	0.03	-0.03	-0.05	-0.08	-0.11	.	.	.	.	.	0.21	0.83	-0.35	-0.57	-0.69	0.54	0.26	-0.26	0.06	0.30
Employment - Ind.	6.03	1.20	0.73	0.14	0.26	0.27	0.17	0.12	.	.	.	.	.	2.36	0.76	0.64	0.55	0.45	0.67	0.70	0.55	0.37	-0.13
Employment - Serv.	3.20	0.64	0.46	-0.02	-0.16	-0.26	-0.17	-0.02	.	.	.	.	.	1.04	0.37	0.13	-0.04	-0.03	0.49	0.66	-0.22	-0.19	-0.34
Employment - P.A.	5.06	1.01	0.78	0.39	0.32	0.01	-0.36	-0.64	.	.	.	.	.	1.02	0.75	-0.41	-0.47	-0.55	0.45	0.81	-0.12	-0.28	-0.43
Real wage - Agr.	5.21	1.04	0.39	0.12	0.31	0.17	-0.06	-0.07	1.71	0.30	0.19	0.17	-0.14	0.95	0.48	-0.04	0.08	0.00	1.08	0.57	0.03	-0.14	-0.06
Real wage - Industry	6.28	1.25	0.29	-0.07	0.11	0.06	0.21	0.23	2.34	0.29	0.01	0.39	0.14	1.26	0.36	-0.58	-0.53	-0.48	0.75	0.64	0.42	0.35	0.17
Real wage - Services	7.09	1.42	0.59	-0.42	-0.44	-0.30	-0.02	0.36	2.30	0.58	-0.19	-0.04	-0.25	1.63	0.41	-0.46	-0.02	0.07	0.57	0.19	-0.02	-0.08	0.07
Real wage - P.A.	7.21	1.44	0.60	-0.17	-0.17	-0.07	0.09	0.36	2.60	0.64	-0.26	-0.10	-0.28	1.60	0.54	-0.19	0.08	0.05	1.21	0.60	0.41	0.22	0.11
Labour productivity	6.09	1.22	0.60	0.04	0.52	0.95	0.61	0.15	.	.	.	.	.	1.00	0.65	0.40	0.80	0.56	0.59	0.67	0.43	0.86	0.60
Solow residual	5.32	1.06	0.09	-0.54	-0.48	0.40	0.51	0.27	.	.	.	.	.	0.87	-0.19	-0.33	0.49	0.31	0.48	-0.02	-0.60	0.32	0.42

Note: the figures refer to HP-filtered annual time series, as described in section 2.2.

Table 2.1b: Time domain summary statistics (1861-1995): first-differences

	Whole sample (1861-1995)								Pre-war					Inter-war					Post-war				
	St.Dev.		Aut.	Correlation with GDP					S.D.	Aut.	Corr. with GDP			S.D.	Aut.	Corr. with GDP			S.D.	Aut.	Corr. with GDP		
	Abs.	Rel.	-1	-2	-1	0	1	2	Rel.	-1	-1	0	1	Rel.	-1	-1	0	1	Rel.	-1	-1	0	1
GDP and expenditure components																							
GDP	5.38	1.00	0.11	-0.02	0.11	1.00	0.11	-0.02	5.14	-0.44	-0.44	1.00	-0.44	5.18	-0.08	-0.08	1.00	-0.08	5.93	0.40	0.40	1.00	0.40
Private Consumption	3.73	0.69	0.37	0.00	0.26	0.62	0.23	0.29	0.50	0.04	-0.03	0.48	0.04	0.72	-0.28	0.34	-0.04	-0.46	0.42	0.46	0.44	0.77	0.32
Investment	21.05	3.91	-0.18	-0.07	-0.18	0.36	0.10	0.03	6.08	-0.52	-0.38	0.47	-0.14	2.84	0.25	0.44	0.01	-0.17	1.13	0.60	0.53	0.79	0.41
Public Consumption	16.20	3.01	0.42	0.10	0.20	0.39	0.04	-0.17	2.59	-0.25	-0.01	0.46	-0.17	4.88	0.22	-0.14	0.55	0.21	0.42	0.29	0.37	0.34	0.41
Exports	30.34	5.64	0.08	-0.09	-0.02	0.52	0.21	-0.04	2.49	-0.22	0.20	-0.23	0.02	4.58	-0.15	0.29	-0.15	-0.27	1.30	0.17	0.27	0.51	0.47
Imports	15.89	2.95	-0.08	-0.11	0.14	0.23	0.33	0.01	2.52	-0.20	0.04	-0.14	0.37	5.70	-0.35	0.28	-0.04	-0.34	1.46	0.15	0.21	0.73	0.35
Net Exports	0.93	0.17	-0.17	0.06	-0.06	0.08	-0.14	0.04	0.15	-0.17	0.01	0.16	-0.44	0.25	-0.32	-0.58	0.26	0.29	0.21	-0.12	0.05	-0.40	0.07
Monetary variables																							
Money stock (M2)	9.98	1.86	0.78	0.09	0.04	-0.05	-0.10	-0.02	1.29	0.32	0.15	0.05	-0.18	1.74	-0.20	0.20	-0.43	0.05	0.86	0.63	0.01	0.11	0.28
GDP deflator	14.03	2.61	0.80	-0.22	-0.25	-0.21	-0.01	0.13	1.22	0.05	-0.18	-0.07	0.05	2.68	0.43	0.17	-0.43	-0.10	1.09	0.88	-0.32	-0.41	-0.63
Money velocity	9.39	1.75	0.25	-0.44	-0.34	0.30	0.17	0.20	1.67	-0.08	-0.47	0.45	-0.02	2.23	-0.06	-0.03	0.27	-0.20	0.95	0.21	-0.19	-0.10	-0.77
Inflation rate	8.93	1.66	0.03	0.04	-0.05	-0.32	-0.22	0.06	1.64	-0.24	-0.14	-0.09	-0.05	2.64	-0.24	0.60	-0.05	-0.37	0.53	0.02	0.27	0.46	-0.25
Wholesale price index	17.54	3.26	0.66	-0.16	-0.15	-0.23	-0.19	0.17	1.22	0.10	-0.23	0.21	0.00	2.60	0.32	0.38	-0.12	-0.12	1.58	0.54	-0.28	-0.24	-0.72
Real interest rate	8.94	1.66	0.04	-0.03	0.06	0.33	0.21	-0.08	1.65	-0.23	0.14	0.09	0.04	2.66	-0.21	-0.59	0.05	0.35	0.48	-0.05	-0.20	-0.48	0.03
Nominal interest rate	0.89	0.17	0.31	0.02	0.12	0.11	-0.12	-0.19	0.10	0.27	0.11	0.13	-0.19	0.15	-0.08	0.08	-0.07	-0.34	0.27	0.43	0.16	0.03	-0.42
Nominal GDP	13.82	2.57	0.74	-0.24	-0.20	0.16	0.04	0.12	1.40	-0.15	-0.43	0.58	-0.19	2.43	0.42	0.12	-0.06	-0.14	0.99	0.69	-0.17	0.00	-0.52
Real money stock	9.34	1.74	0.39	0.43	0.41	0.26	-0.09	-0.22	1.51	0.07	0.27	0.10	-0.20	2.19	0.01	0.00	0.18	0.17	1.09	0.58	0.33	0.50	0.84
Budget expenditures	16.21	3.01	0.49	-0.03	0.01	0.14	0.08	0.18	2.48	-0.36	-0.06	0.41	-0.24	3.15	0.33	-0.15	0.02	0.32	2.05	0.08	-0.22	-0.19	-0.26
Budget revenues	15.04	2.80	0.69	-0.21	-0.18	0.16	0.34	0.13	1.34	0.12	-0.09	0.17	0.14	2.73	0.36	-0.45	-0.29	0.43	1.45	0.38	-0.29	-0.15	-0.23
Labour market variables																							
Employment - Total	1.56	0.29	0.47	0.18	0.14	0.04	-0.16	-0.14	.	.	.	.	.	0.57	0.52	0.27	-0.02	-0.10	0.18	0.20	0.23	0.34	0.10
Employment - Agr.	2.33	2.33	0.42	-0.11	-0.12	-0.09	-0.09	-0.10	.	.	.	.	.	0.27	0.84	-0.44	-0.43	-0.12	0.46	-0.12	-0.11	0.08	0.11
Employment - Ind.	4.97	4.97	0.40	0.17	0.16	0.14	-0.05	0.03	.	.	.	.	.	2.07	0.44	0.50	0.22	0.00	0.44	0.58	0.70	0.67	0.25
Employment - Serv.	4.15	4.15	0.24	0.09	-0.07	-0.19	-0.09	0.07	.	.	.	.	.	1.68	0.09	-0.01	-0.32	-0.16	0.30	0.26	-0.19	-0.03	-0.26
Employment - P.A.	3.93	3.93	0.56	0.13	0.30	0.05	-0.23	-0.53	.	.	.	.	.	0.85	0.07	0.00	0.16	-0.07	0.24	0.62	0.35	0.24	0.14
Real wage - Industry	6.42	1.19	0.00	0.17	0.33	0.15	-0.11	-0.03	1.37	-0.22	0.12	0.19	-0.18	1.60	-0.22	-0.26	0.50	0.11	0.91	0.53	0.20	-0.09	-0.03
Real wage - Industry	7.81	1.45	-0.16	0.00	0.23	-0.10	0.18	0.14	1.70	0.21	0.04	0.46	-0.10	1.72	-0.23	-0.34	-0.19	0.02	0.54	0.41	0.46	0.30	0.11
Real wage - Services	7.16	1.33	0.21	-0.07	-0.13	-0.07	-0.03	0.35	1.31	0.21	0.16	0.25	-0.10	2.10	-0.15	-0.60	0.09	0.12	0.58	0.35	0.41	0.20	0.42
Real wage - P.A.	7.20	1.34	0.21	0.00	-0.04	0.01	0.00	0.33	1.37	0.24	0.14	0.23	-0.08	1.95	-0.11	-0.51	0.14	-0.01	0.68	0.05	0.24	0.02	0.06
Labour productivity	6.10	1.13	0.27	-0.14	0.21	0.97	0.28	-0.06	.	.	.	.	.	1.16	0.00	-0.24	0.87	-0.02	0.42	0.43	0.34	0.92	0.46
Solow residual	7.27	1.35	-0.27	-0.28	-0.63	0.58	0.28	-0.01	.	.	.	.	.	1.37	-0.04	-0.84	0.28	0.29	0.45	-0.45	-0.60	0.45	0.13

Note: the figures refer to first differences of annual time series, as described in section 2.2.

Table 2.2a: Time domain summary statistics: G7 (HP-filtered)

	Whole sample (1861-1995)								Pre-war				Inter-war				Post-war			
	St.Dev.		Aut.	Correlation with ITA-GDP					S.D.	Corr. with ITA-GD			S.D.	Corr. with ITA-GD			S.D.	Corr. with ITA-GD		
	Abs.	Rel.	-1	-2	-1	0	1	2	Rel.	-1	0	1	Rel.	-1	0	1	Rel.	-1	0	1
Deviations from HP trend																				
Italy	5.01	1.00	0.52	0.10	0.52	1.00	0.52	0.10	2.66	-0.09	1.00	-0.09	4.89	0.73	1.00	0.73	3.17	0.54	1.00	0.54
USA	6.53	1.30	0.64	0.33	0.24	-0.07	-0.33	-0.40	1.79	0.09	-0.07	-0.12	2.08	0.40	0.39	0.29	0.73	0.03	0.31	0.37
Japan	4.39	0.88	0.57	0.15	0.36	0.39	0.27	0.08	1.57	0.18	-0.04	-0.11	1.29	0.22	0.33	0.40	0.80	0.42	0.55	0.44
Germany	4.35	0.87	0.72	0.14	0.17	0.18	0.19	0.15	1.22	-0.16	-0.08	0.05	1.77	0.38	0.47	0.55	0.91	0.06	-0.11	-0.29
France	4.50	0.90	0.60	-0.09	-0.06	-0.01	-0.11	-0.15	1.42	-0.31	0.02	-0.11	1.79	0.20	0.15	-0.05	0.50	0.12	0.31	0.21
UK	4.03	0.80	0.62	0.36	0.52	0.50	0.21	-0.09	0.94	0.02	0.16	-0.06	1.01	0.59	0.57	0.50	0.68	-0.06	0.20	0.24
Canada	5.83	1.16	0.56	0.31	0.28	0.13	-0.15	-0.28	1.96	0.00	0.04	-0.25	2.07	0.45	0.34	0.19	0.74	-0.03	0.15	0.12

Note: the figures refer to HP-filtered annual time series, as described in section 2.2.

Table 2.2b: Time domain summary statistics: G7 (first differences)

	Whole sample (1861-1995)								Pre-war				Inter-war				Post-war			
	St.Dev.		Aut.	Correlation with ITA-GDP					S.D.	Corr. with ITA-GD			S.D.	Corr. with ITA-GD			S.D.	Corr. with ITA-GD		
	Abs.	Rel.	-1	-2	-1	0	1	2	Rel.	-1	0	1	Rel.	-1	0	1	Rel.	-1	0	1
Growth rates																				
Italy	5.38	1.00	0.11	-0.02	0.11	1.00	0.11	-0.02	4.14	-0.44	1.00	-0.44	4.18	-0.08	1.00	-0.08	4.93	0.40	1.00	0.40
USA	5.99	1.11	0.24	0.17	0.23	-0.09	-0.28	-0.24	1.33	0.12	-0.08	-0.03	1.99	0.37	0.53	0.12	0.52	0.01	0.44	0.43
Japan	4.75	0.88	0.21	0.06	0.28	0.30	0.17	0.02	1.12	0.28	-0.18	-0.15	1.40	-0.11	0.06	0.28	0.65	0.48	0.62	0.62
Germany	4.00	0.74	0.44	0.10	0.11	0.10	0.16	0.15	0.75	-0.07	-0.03	0.08	1.74	0.26	0.12	0.40	0.63	0.28	0.38	0.22
France	4.91	0.91	0.22	-0.01	-0.02	0.13	-0.05	0.03	1.16	-0.24	0.26	-0.16	1.70	0.26	0.41	0.09	0.38	0.40	0.63	0.41
UK	3.77	0.70	0.12	0.16	0.26	0.35	0.04	-0.01	0.82	0.05	0.18	-0.33	1.21	0.33	0.49	0.38	0.42	-0.03	0.35	0.37
Canada	5.88	1.09	0.08	0.19	0.16	0.15	-0.13	-0.07	1.68	-0.01	0.20	-0.20	1.85	0.30	0.49	0.23	0.54	0.18	0.45	0.33

Note: the figures refer to growth rates of annual time series, as described in section 2.2.

Table 2.3: GDP volatility by source and sub-period

	1861-1889	1890-1914	1922-1939	1951-1973	1974-1992	1861-1914	1922-1939	1951-1992	1861-1992
					First differences				
ISTAT	3.02	4.20	4.19	1.83	2.08	3.65	4.19	2.35	6.54
Fuà	3.24	4.04	3.73	1.72	2.10	3.67	3.73	2.33	6.30
Maddison	3.53	4.20	3.82	1.47	2.10	3.91	3.82	2.22	5.45
Toniolo	3.24	4.74	3.13	1.49	2.09	4.07	3.13	2.22	5.35
Chain Index	3.43	4.19	4.41	1.63	2.24	3.87	4.41	2.34	5.91
					Deviations from HP trend				
ISTAT	1.95	2.76	5.39	2.26	1.84	2.34	5.39	2.10	6.32
Fuà	2.10	3.08	5.26	1.95	1.86	2.60	5.26	1.93	5.88
Maddison	2.37	3.06	4.86	1.70	1.85	2.73	4.86	1.78	5.29
Toniolo	2.09	3.20	4.34	1.71	1.85	2.65	4.34	1.79	5.01
Chain Index	2.32	2.91	5.42	2.33	2.00	2.59	5.42	2.20	5.89

Note: the figures reported are standard deviations (see section 2.2 for details on sources).

Table 2.4: Test statistics for the null hypothesis of constant volatility

Null Hypothesis	Post-Unity = Giolitti	Giolitti = Interwar	Interwar = Boom	Boom = Post-Oil	PreWWI = InterWW	InterWW = PostWWII	PreWWI = PostWWII	PreWWII = PostWWII	PreWWI = InterWW = PostWWII
					First differences				
ISTAT	1.93 *	1.01	5.23 **	1.30	1.32	3.19 **	2.42 **	2.63 **	23.66 **
Fua'	1.55	1.17	4.70 **	1.49	1.03	2.56 **	2.48 **	2.50 **	23.68 **
Maddison	1.41	1.20	6.72 **	2.02 *	0.96	2.97 **	3.11 **	3.07 **	22.44 **
Toniolo	2.14 *	2.29 **	4.45 **	1.99 *	0.59	1.99 **	3.36 **	3.05 **	26.03 **
Chain Index	1.49	0.90	7.28 **	1.88 *	1.30	3.55 **	2.73 **	2.91 **	24.58 **
					Deviations from HP trend				
ISTAT	2.01 **	3.82 **	5.67 **	1.51	5.30 **	6.60 **	1.25	2.63 **	33.35 **
Fua'	2.16 *	2.92 **	7.31 **	1.10	4.09 **	7.44 **	1.82 **	3.16 **	29.25 **
Maddison	1.66	2.52 **	8.16 **	0.85	3.18 **	7.43 **	2.34 **	3.54 **	26.18 **
Toniolo	2.34 **	1.84 *	6.48 **	0.85	2.68 **	5.90 **	2.20 **	3.07 **	20.00 **
Chain Index	1.56	3.48 **	5.40 **	1.36	4.38 **	6.05 **	1.38	2.49 **	25.13 **

Note: the figures reported are F-test statistics. The last column reports Bartlett test statistics. Single and double asterisks indicate significance at the 5 and 1 per cent level, respectively. See section 2.2 for details on the tests.

Table 2.5: Volatility of GDP components

	1861-1889	1890-1914	1922-1939	1951-1973	1974-1992	1861-1914	1922-1939	1951-1992	1861-1992
					Decomposition by formation				
Agriculture	1.90	2.23	3.71	3.46	1.92	2.07	3.71	2.08	1.64
Industry	1.58	1.08	2.24	2.26	1.74	1.28	2.24	1.91	1.65
Services	1.33	0.72	1.02	1.08	0.92	0.96	1.02	0.95	1.45
					Decomposition by use				
Private Cons.	0.59	0.42	0.85	1.21	0.80	0.50	0.85	0.94	0.69
Public Cons.	3.54	1.91	4.80	1.60	0.38	2.59	4.80	0.94	3.01
Fixed Cap.Form.	10.07	1.81	3.52	3.59	1.87	6.08	3.52	2.51	3.91
Inventories	44.94	35.93	23.46	55.60	29.04	38.39	23.46	32.68	21.76
Net Exports	8.03	4.88	12.50	25.43	50.96	6.04	12.50	34.24	9.51

Note: the figures reported are standard deviations of log-differenced series. Turning points identified on HP-filtered series with the TP5 procedure (see section 2.5).

Table 2.6: Growth cycle chronology - Rossi-Fuà GDP

Turning points				Duration				Amplitude			
T-year	P-year	Trough	Peak	T-T	P-P	Exp.	Cont.	T-T	P-P	Exp.	Cont.
1863	1862	-2.1	1.3	.	.	.	1	.	.	.	3.3
1867	1866	-3.3	6.8	4	4	3	1	18.9	12.1	8.8	10.1
1874	1873	-1.7	1.1	7	7	6	1	7.3	14.5	4.4	2.9
1881	1880	-3.7	2.4	7	7	6	1	10.3	7.0	4.1	6.1
1889	1886	-4.0	2.4	8	6	5	3	12.5	12.3	6.1	6.4
1892	1891	-3.5	4.5	3	5	2	1	16.5	14.8	8.5	8.0
1897	1896	-4.7	1.3	5	5	4	1	10.9	12.9	4.9	6.0
1899	1898	-6.2	0.6	2	2	1	1	9.7	10.1	4.1	5.6
1906	1901	-2.4	4.5	7	3	2	5	17.6	16.3	10.7	6.9
1910	1907	-7.3	4.5	4	6	1	3	18.6	13.8	6.9	11.7
1920	1918	-9.1	18.4	10	11	8	2	53.2	37.4	25.7	27.5
1934	1929	-4.9	4.1	14	11	9	5	22.1	40.6	13.2	9.0
1945	1939	-34.8	11.5	11	10	5	6	62.6	25.3	16.3	46.3
1958	1953	-1.1	3.0	13	14	8	5	41.9	84.1	37.8	4.1
1965	1962	-2.9	2.0	7	9	4	3	8.0	7.3	3.1	4.9
1972	1970	-1.4	2.7	7	8	5	2	9.8	10.6	5.7	4.1
1975	1974	-3.6	2.5	3	4	2	1	10.1	8.0	3.9	6.2
1983	1980	-2.3	3.5	8	6	5	3	12.9	13.3	7.2	5.8
1993	1990	-2.6	2.1	10	10	7	3	9.0	10.2	4.4	4.66
Average (overall)		-5.3	4.2	7.2	7.1	4.6	2.5	19.5	19.5	9.8	9.4
Average (pre-war)		-3.9	2.9	5.2	5.0	3.3	1.8	13.6	12.6	6.5	6.7
Average (inter-war)		-19.8	7.8	12.5	10.5	7.0	5.5	42.4	33.0	14.7	27.6
Average (post-war)		-2.3	2.6	8.0	8.5	5.2	2.8	15.3	22.2	10.3	5.0

Note: turning point dates were identified with the TP5 procedure (see section 2.5).

Table 2.7: Growth cycle chronology - Chain Index GDP

Turning points				Duration				Amplitude			
T-year	P-year	Trough	Peak	T-T	P-P	Exp.	Cont.	T-T	P-P	Exp.	Cont.
1863	1862	-2.7	0.5	.	.	.	1	.	.	.	3.2
1867	1866	-4.6	6.4	4	4	3	1	20.0	12.2	9.0	11.0
1872	1870	-2.6	0.8	5	4	3	2	8.9	16.4	5.4	3.4
1881	1875	-5.0	2.3	9	5	3	6	12.2	8.3	4.9	7.3
1889	1886	-4.2	2.1	8	11	5	3	13.3	14.4	7.1	6.2
1897	1891	-6.8	3.7	8	5	2	6	18.4	14.1	7.9	10.5
1906	1901	-2.8	5.0	9	10	4	5	19.6	22.3	11.8	7.8
1910	1907	-5.1	4.1	4	6	1	3	16.1	14.7	7.0	9.2
1919	1916	-6.6	9.4	9	9	6	3	30.4	23.6	14.4	16.0
1922	1920	-9.0	2.1	3	4	1	2	19.8	24.7	8.7	11.1
1927	1925	-2.1	2.5	5	5	3	2	16.0	22.5	11.5	4.6
1934	1929	-5.7	4.9	7	4	2	5	17.6	11.5	7.0	10.7
1945	1940	-43.7	14.6	11	11	6	5	78.6	30.9	20.3	58.3
1958	1951	-1.6	7.0	13	11	6	7	59.3	108.9	50.7	8.6
1965	1962	-2.6	1.8	7	11	4	3	7.8	12.1	3.4	4.4
1972	1970	-1.4	1.5	7	8	5	2	6.9	8.5	4.1	2.9
1975	1974	-3.7	3.2	3	4	2	1	11.4	7.4	4.6	6.9
1983	1980	-2.5	3.5	8	6	5	3	13.2	14.1	7.2	6.0
1993	1990	-2.5	2.3	10	10	7	3	9.5	10.7	4.7	4.81
Average (overall)		-6.1	4.1	7.2	7.1	3.8	3.3	21.1	21.0	10.5	10.1
Average (pre-war)		-4.2	3.1	6.7	6.4	3.0	3.4	15.5	14.6	7.6	7.3
Average (inter-war)		-5.6	3.2	5.0	4.3	2.0	3.0	17.8	19.6	9.1	8.8
Average (post-war)		-2.4	3.2	8.0	8.3	4.8	3.2	18.0	26.9	12.4	5.6

Note: turning point dates were identified with the TP5 procedure (see section 2.5).

Table 2.8: Comovements by cycle and phase - HP detrended

		Consumption			Investment			Public Expenditure		
Trough	Peak	Exp.	Cont.	Cyc-Cor.	Exp.	Cont.	Cyc-Cor.	Exp.	Cont.	Cyc-Cor.
1863	1866	4.05	-1.25	0.91	30.30	-21.60	0.52	37.68	-1.40	0.92
1867	1870	1.94	-5.27	0.93	9.23	-29.03	0.58	16.35	-43.69	0.97
1872	1875	3.64	-1.30	0.23	12.69	-2.88	0.69	5.78	-12.14	0.34
1881	1886	-0.39	-2.00	-0.13	91.12	-59.24	0.84	5.05	-8.21	0.19
1889	1891	4.12	-0.66	0.59	25.26	-66.49	0.57	-3.75	8.14	-0.75
1897	1901	2.52	-5.20	0.73	8.68	-3.27	0.31	3.42	5.76	0.18
1906	1907	2.86	-1.27	0.86	8.11	7.88	0.33	-6.53	-8.99	-0.11
1910	1916	3.21	-3.74	0.42	-59.69	2.17	-0.63	99.54	-15.44	0.67
1919	1920	5.79	-6.24	-0.06	14.81	36.74	-0.96	-59.20	-25.72	0.95
1922	1925	1.03	-1.76	0.26	27.57	-13.04	0.56	-24.69	0.90	-0.72
1927	1929	2.16	1.19	0.81	4.03	-16.70	-0.30	2.92	22.80	0.48
1934	1940	11.59	-5.36	0.84	35.81	-22.41	0.85	9.41	-2.06	0.19
1945	1951	24.92	-32.50	0.82	78.95	-104.45	0.80	-0.89	-5.20	0.14
1958	1962	2.28	-4.64	0.85	9.26	-1.00	0.68	-0.87	8.70	-0.45
1965	1970	3.44	-1.30	0.72	14.61	-16.88	0.93	-0.75	-1.29	0.24
1972	1974	1.51	-2.48	0.88	6.20	-4.91	0.90	-1.45	2.91	-0.78
1975	1980	6.47	-3.58	0.93	10.14	-8.74	0.80	-0.44	-0.60	0.26
1983	1990	2.34	-5.58	0.95	9.08	-12.12	0.97	-0.06	0.29	-0.03

		Exports			Imports			Employment		
Trough	Peak	Exp.	Cont.	Cyc-Cor.	Exp.	Cont.	Cyc-Cor.	Exp.	Cont.	Cyc-Cor.
1863	1866	-18.07	10.28	-0.73	-9.24	13.53	-0.47	.	.	.
1867	1870	-8.96	7.47	-0.47	-1.81	-3.16	0.52	.	.	.
1872	1875	-8.99	18.27	0.17	4.18	11.07	0.13	.	.	.
1881	1886	-9.99	5.43	-0.15	8.03	-8.46	0.04	.	.	.
1889	1891	-20.82	7.41	-0.67	-29.30	4.51	-0.48	.	.	.
1897	1901	0.19	13.07	-0.50	14.03	8.21	0.06	.	.	.
1906	1907	-3.17	8.87	-0.44	4.62	0.56	0.55	6.89	-6.93	1.00
1910	1916	-2.90	3.42	-0.39	11.03	-6.37	0.27	7.14	-11.69	0.57
1919	1920	24.62	-14.35	-0.78	22.85	-14.25	-0.71	-0.20	-0.08	-0.45
1922	1925	30.00	-22.76	0.35	30.24	-43.22	-0.21	8.93	-5.42	0.30
1927	1929	9.55	-14.01	0.25	23.62	-8.87	0.98	-1.02	1.61	-0.59
1934	1940	39.84	-31.61	0.70	23.94	-34.96	0.47	3.72	-6.48	0.47
1945	1951	276.52	-265.20	0.90	52.27	-57.07	0.53	-3.03	-0.60	0.13
1958	1962	5.79	-41.30	0.67	18.72	-21.48	0.84	1.39	3.06	-0.33
1965	1970	0.68	0.93	0.15	15.36	-12.44	0.78	0.37	-2.59	0.58
1972	1974	-2.56	-0.76	-0.20	0.15	-2.48	0.49	2.43	-1.95	0.95
1975	1980	2.89	-4.64	0.30	15.49	-17.89	0.96	1.67	-0.83	0.83
1983	1990	10.16	-3.01	0.47	13.26	-13.43	0.82	0.00	-1.27	0.70

		GDP deflator			Money stock			Real wage (ind.)		
Trough	Peak	Exp.	Cont.	Cyc-Cor.	Exp.	Cont.	Cyc-Cor.	Exp.	Cont.	Cyc-Cor.
1863	1866	1.25	-7.21	0.15	4.40	-6.07	0.33	.	.	.
1867	1870	-3.87	0.87	-0.25	-8.11	0.53	0.15	.	.	.
1872	1875	-12.33	10.43	-0.24	-11.43	16.27	-0.30	.	.	.
1881	1886	4.87	4.83	0.23	7.88	-4.73	0.39	.	.	.
1889	1891	2.70	-1.20	0.18	-4.56	-0.62	-0.50	.	.	.
1897	1901	1.68	-5.94	-0.24	2.99	-3.45	-0.08	8.79	-11.85	0.42
1906	1907	0.83	4.45	0.05	4.04	3.58	0.02	1.03	-0.88	-0.11
1910	1916	-18.82	-2.77	-0.20	-22.59	-4.31	-0.16	-9.34	-4.47	-0.04
1919	1920	24.48	22.26	-0.80	4.92	43.04	-0.63	-3.50	13.33	-0.19
1922	1925	6.73	-19.24	-0.63	2.18	-25.91	-0.85	-10.59	3.64	-0.34
1927	1929	-2.98	-8.63	-0.69	0.02	-0.22	-0.41	-7.55	7.60	-0.67
1934	1940	-22.94	-13.21	-0.67	-22.90	-6.08	-0.84	14.42	10.63	0.07
1945	1951	-13.28	53.63	-0.42	8.77	26.93	-0.28	-0.56	-15.74	0.30
1958	1962	3.23	-17.14	0.59	9.99	-19.12	0.87	4.73	-8.83	0.90
1965	1970	-10.90	9.19	-0.86	-9.26	-0.43	-0.52	2.68	-0.77	0.27
1972	1974	6.95	-6.00	0.82	0.11	2.31	-0.07	0.15	-2.22	0.24
1975	1980	5.23	1.53	0.18	8.25	3.54	0.36	-0.67	0.55	-0.06
1983	1990	-12.42	6.45	-0.59	-7.27	-1.10	-0.06	1.11	-1.73	0.56

Note: the statistics displayed in the table are, for selected variables, the phase-specific change (relative to trend) and the cycle-specific correlation with GDP.

Table 2.9: Cross-cycle averages of cyclical statistics:

		Dur.	Amp.	Cyclical correlations						
Country	Sample	GDP		C	I	G	NX	M	P	INF
Australia	1861-1996	7.06	23.03	0.37	0.21	0.41	-0.23	0.30	0.24	-0.05
Canada	1870-1996	7.50	25.47	0.08	0.56	0.29	-0.11	0.36	0.09	0.20
Denmark	1870-1996	7.19	19.54	.	0.69	.	.	-0.16	-0.53	-0.24
Germany	1850-1996	9.23	38.25	0.94	0.69	0.93	0.07	0.65	-0.10	-0.04
Italy	1861-1996	7.06	21.26	0.84	0.45	-0.01	-0.05	-0.18	-0.14	-0.53
Japan	1885-1996	8.08	25.64	0.92	0.75	0.51	0.03	0.62	0.75	0.39
Norway	1865-1996	7.93	16.52	0.76	0.66	0.14	0.00	0.01	0.03	0.15
Sweden	1861-1996	6.58	11.80	0.76	0.59	-0.06	0.09	-0.41	-0.41	-0.02
United Kingdom	1870-1996	7.53	16.22	0.56	0.33	0.26	-0.10	0.14	-0.17	0.32
United States	1869-1996	6.94	26.81	0.74	0.24	0.62	-0.25	0.50	0.09	0.20
Cross-country average		7.51	22.45	0.66	0.52	0.34	-0.06	0.18	-0.02	0.04
Standard Deviation		0.76	7.35	0.28	0.20	0.31	0.12	0.36	0.36	0.28

Note: the figures reported are averages of cycle-specific statistics for HP filtered data. See section 2.7 for a description of the statistics reported and the data sources.

Table 2.10: Measures of cross-cycle variability

	Dur.	Amp.	Cyclical correlations							Steepness
Country	GDP		C	I	G	NX	M	P	INF	Exp - Con
Australia	3.26	12.84	0.60	0.49	0.64	0.45	0.52	0.64	0.54	0.28
Canada	2.88	16.67	0.56	0.49	0.61	0.51	0.49	0.50	0.49	0.32
Denmark	2.29	12.22	.	0.12	.	.	0.56	0.54	0.52	0.95
Germany	4.36	34.57	0.46	0.54	0.61	0.35	0.48	0.46	0.32	2.14
Italy	3.75	20.21	0.22	0.44	0.44	0.50	0.50	0.34	0.53	0.88
Japan	5.45	25.80	0.47	0.54	0.64	0.39	0.64	0.70	0.65	1.77
Norway	3.28	10.74	0.23	0.28	0.46	0.46	0.59	0.66	0.32	1.13
Sweden	2.59	5.80	0.21	0.36	0.55	0.34	0.51	0.57	0.44	1.04
United Kingdom	2.95	9.91	0.52	0.63	0.62	0.58	0.61	0.63	0.48	1.21
United States	3.04	16.87	0.18	0.61	0.58	0.39	0.42	0.61	0.49	0.75

Note: the figures reported are cross-cycle standard deviations, except for column 10 (average differences). See section 2.7 for a description of the statistics and data sources.

Table 2.11: Tests of the representative cycle hypothesis (p-values)

	Dur.	Amp.	Cyclical correlations							Steepness
Country	GDP		C	I	G	NX	M	P	INF	Exp - Con
Australia	0.08	0.00	0.21	0.75	0.03	0.60	0.19	0.01	0.03	0.27
Canada	0.51	0.01	0.07	0.27	0.09	0.26	0.20	0.58	0.19	0.44
Denmark	0.71	0.11	.	0.99	.	.	0.08	0.27	0.17	0.06
Germany	0.08	0.00	0.01	0.02	0.00	0.81	0.13	0.69	0.80	0.00
Italy	0.00	0.01	0.55	0.22	0.91	0.18	0.61	0.94	0.51	0.04
Japan	0.04	0.18	0.00	0.09	0.01	0.75	0.01	0.00	0.00	0.02
Norway	0.06	0.00	0.75	0.62	0.72	0.75	0.09	0.01	1.00	0.03
Sweden	0.42	0.41	0.80	0.44	0.50	0.99	0.56	0.27	0.82	0.00
United Kingdom	0.25	0.02	0.25	0.06	0.06	0.16	0.01	0.00	0.14	0.03
United States	0.09	0.00	0.77	0.90	0.06	0.76	0.61	0.16	0.37	0.05

Note: the figures reported are p-values (see section 2.7 for a description of the tests).

Figure 2.1: GDP index: growth rate by sub-period

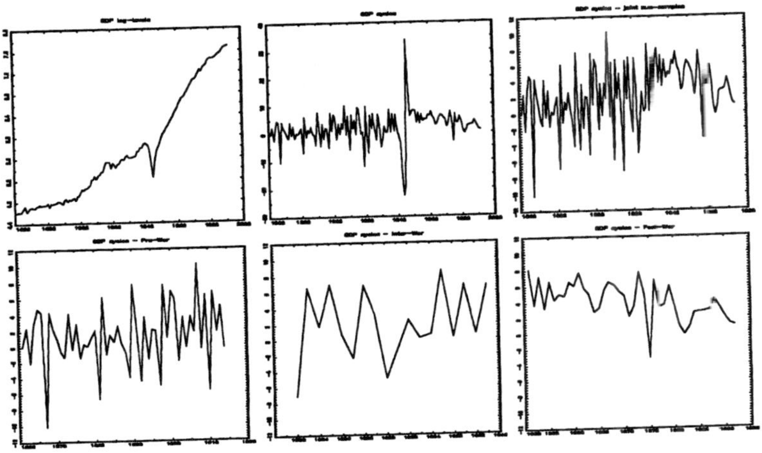

Figure 2.2: GDP index: deviation from HP trend by sub-period

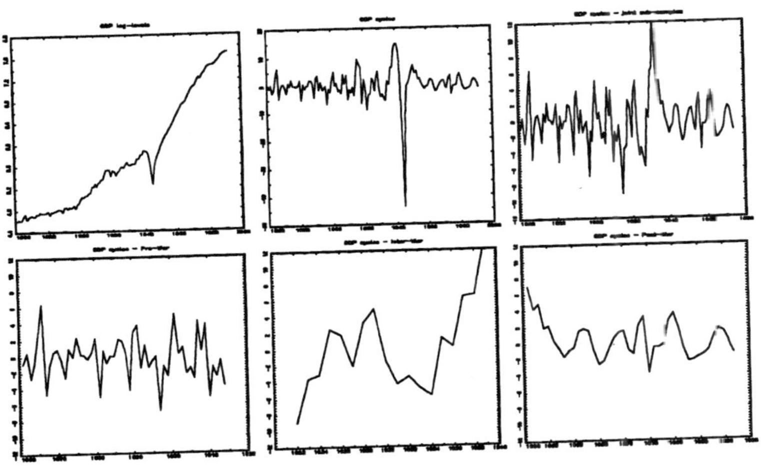

Figure 2.3 GDP Supply components (relative share)

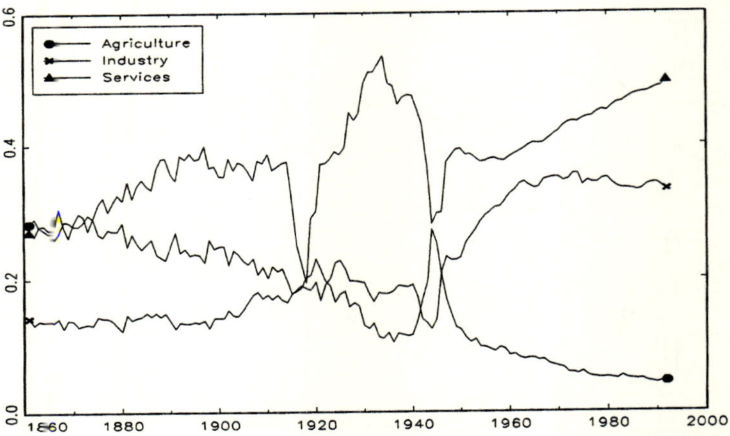

Figure 2.4: GDP Demand components (relative share)

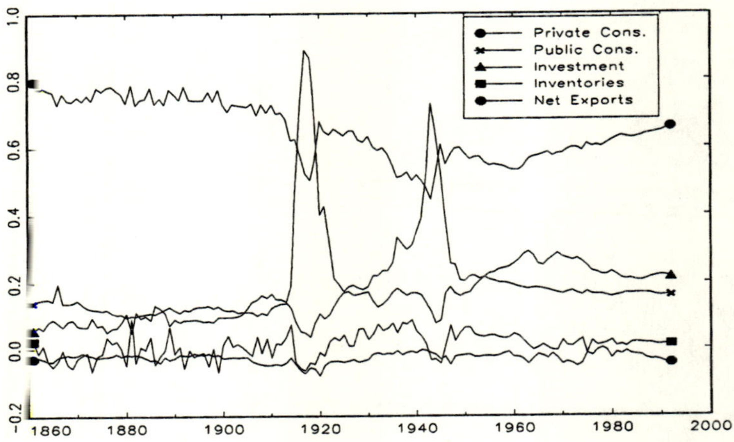

Figure 2.5: Cyclical component of GDP (Rossi-Fuà and FG Chain Index)

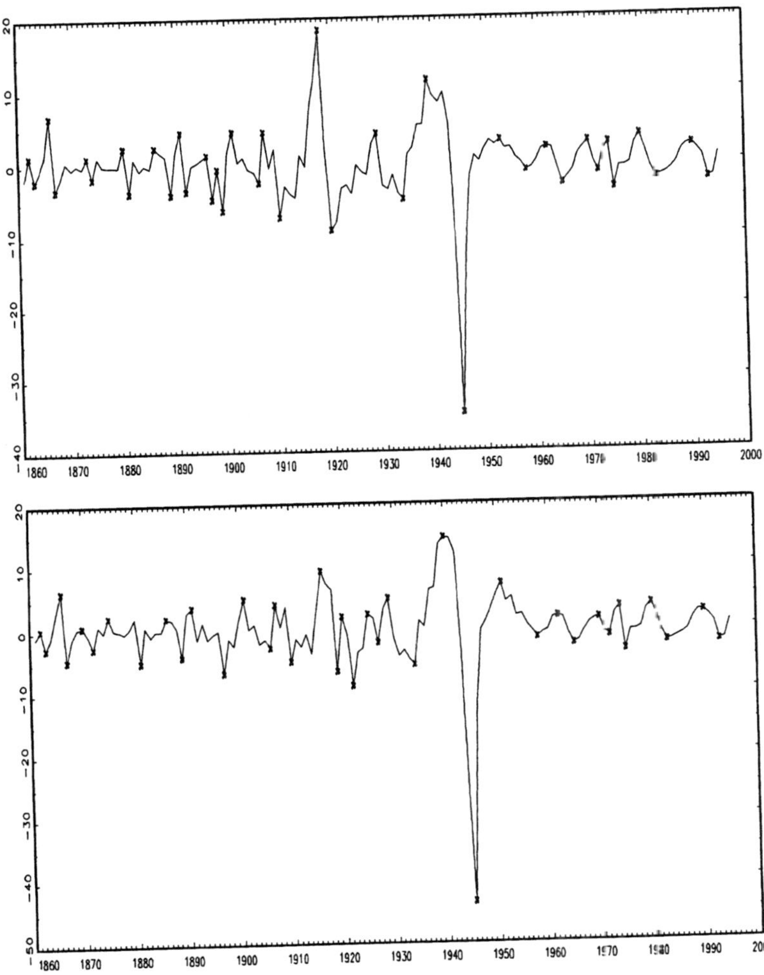

Chapter 3

Asymmetries and Non-linearities in Aggregate Fluctuations

3.1 Introduction

Aggregate fluctuations are commonly interpreted within the Frisch-Slutsky analytical approach: random shocks (the *impulses*) affect output through distributed-lag relations (the *propagation mechanism*). Within this framework it is generally assumed, as a reasonable approximation, that the propagation mechanism is linear and that the disturbances follow a gaussian distribution. These two assumptions, however, impose strong restrictions on the behaviour of economic time series. In particular, they imply a symmetric behaviour over the business cycle. Asymmetric cyclical time series cannot be generated by linear gaussian models (see e.g. Blatt, 1980; Potter, 1995).

The presence of systematic business cycle asymmetries (henceforth BCA), however, would have a number of important implications: theoretical business cycle models should incorporate asymmetric behaviour; linear forecasting models which ignore information about the state of the economy would be inefficient; the design and implementation of stabilization policies would have to be conditional on the stage of the cycle.

The idea that the behaviour of economic systems may be different across the phases of a business cycle was already present in the work of Mitchell (1927), Keynes (1936), and Hicks (1950). More recently, a number of studies have reconsidered this issue, with a focus on either testing for (e.g. Neftci, 1984; DeLong and Summers, 1986; McQueen and Thorley, 1993) or modelling business cycle asymmetries (e.g. Hamilton, 1989; Terasvirta and Anderson, 1992; Potter, 1995).

This chapter reports the results of an empirical investigation of business cycle asymmetries in the Italian economy.[1] Our study contributes to the existing literature in three respects. First, no such analyses have been reported so far for the Italian economy. Second, we present evidence not only for quarterly post-war time series, as it is common in the literature, but also for annual long-run time series (1861-1992). Third, we consider explicitly the relationship between asymmetries and non-linearities.[2]

Our results are twofold. On the one hand, consistently with the existing literature, we find that non-parametric tests provide only limited evidence of asymmetries. On the other hand, we show that business cycle asymmetries are sufficient to account for the finding of neglected non-linearities in macroeconomic time series. This finding indicates that cyclical asymmetries provide not only an intuitive economic interpretation but also a *parsimonious* representation of non-linearities in economic time series.

The chapter is structured as follows. Section 3.2 describes the data set and presents the evidence on the presence of non-linearity in Italian macroeconomic time series. Section 3.3 reports the results of asymmetry tests, while in section 3.4 we apply threshold autoregressive and Markov-switching models to characterize the asymmetric behaviour of recessions and expansions. Section 3.5 examines whether the finding of neglected non-linearity can be accounted for by cyclical asymmetries. Section 3.6 concludes with the implications of the analysis and some directions for future research.

---

[1]Recent related works include Mills (1995) and Holly and Stannett (1995) for the UK, Peel and Speight (1996) for the US, and Westlund and Ohlen (1991) for Sweden.

[2]This chapter draws on Stanca (1999c).

3.2 Non-Linearities in Macroeconomic Time Series

Two sets of Italian macroeconomic time series are investigated in the following: first, time series spanning the whole post-Unity period (1861-1992) at annual frequency (from Rossi *et al.*, 1993, and ISTAT, 1986), henceforth referred to as *long* for brevity; second, time series spanning part of the post-war period (1960-1995) at quarterly frequency (from the OECD Main Economic Indicators database), henceforth referred to as *short*. Each of the two sets includes five macroeconomic variables expressed at constant prices: Gross Domestic Product, Private Consumption, Gross Investment, Exports, and Imports of goods and services. The reason for analysing two partially overlapping data sets, at different frequencies, is to strike a balance in the trade-off between the features which are desirable for business cycle analysis. The *long* series provide information on more cycles, and are in this sense the most natural choice, but imply the cost of fewer observations per cycle and lower data quality. The *short* series provide more accurate information on individual cycles and are more reliable, at the cost of covering just a few cyclical episodes.

The log-transformed series were made stationary by first differencing.[3] We also experimented with fourth differencing on the quarterly series, in order to obtain smoother annual growth rates directly comparable with the *long* series, but the results of the analysis were virtually unchanged. The resulting cyclical components can be given an economic interpretation in the light of the view, shared by Schumpeter (1939), Kaldor (1954), and Goodwin (1955), that business cycles are an intrinsic element of the growth process, and that an integrated theory of cyclical economic development is thus required. In this view, the growth process is itself cyclical, and the business cycle is naturally identified with observed movements in the growth rates of economic activity.

All series were checked for the presence of identifiable outliers. As a result, the observations corresponding to the world war II period (1939-1946) for the *long* series were adjusted by means of corresponding dummy variables.

---

[3]The results of unit root tests for the log-differenced series led to the rejection of the non-stationarity null in all cases.

Each series was then whitened by fitting an appropriate autoregressive model, with the order of the autoregression being selected on the basis of the Akaike Information Criterion (AIC).[4] Descriptive statistics for both the raw series and the residuals from the fitted autoregressive models are displayed in table 3.1. The residuals from the fitted linear models were then subjected to a series of non-linearity tests.[5] Both diagnostic tests and tests for linearity against specific alternatives were performed. Two different diagnostic tests were used. The first is the *portmanteau* test statistic by McLeod and Li (1983), which is based on the autocorrelation function of the squared values of the residuals from the fitted linear autoregressive models. The second is the BDS test (see e.g. Brock *et al.*, 1996), a statistic based on the correlation dimension of the residuals from the fitted linear autoregressive model.

In addition to diagnostic statistics, we considered LM tests of linearity against the following non-linear alternatives: Autoregressive Conditional Heteroskedasticity (ARCH), Smooth Transition Autoregression (STAR), and Bilinearity (BL). For each of these tests, the corresponding LM statistic is obtained as the number of observations times the coefficient of determination from an auxiliary regression where the residuals from the linear model are regressed on appropriately augmented sets of regressors.[6] The Lagrange Multiplier (LM) test for ARCH effects (Engle, 1982; Weiss, 1986) is based on the test statistic $Q = nR^2$ from the regression

$$\hat{\varepsilon}_t^2 = \alpha_0 + \sum_{i=1}^{p} \alpha_i \hat{\varepsilon}_{t-i}^2 + \eta_t \tag{3.1}$$

Under the null hypothesis of linearity, the Q statistic is asymptotically distributed as χ^2 with p degrees of freedom.[7] The LM test of linearity against STAR developed by Luukkonen *et al.* (1988), was computed in three different

[4]The results did not change substantially when the more conservative Schwarz (1978) information criterion was used.

[5]For a detailed discussion of linearity tests, which is beyond the scope of this work, see Granger and Terasvirta (1993) and Tong (1990). Lee *et al.* (1993) investigate empirically the relative advantages of the most recent testing techniques.

[6]The intuition behind this type of tests is that if the addition of non-linear terms helps to explain the variability of the residuals from the linear model, the null of linearity can be rejected against the specific alternative implied by the nature of the additional regressors.

[7]It should be noted that this test is asymptotically equivalent to the McLeod-Li portmanteau statistic.

versions, depending on the set of additional regressors to be included in the auxiliary regressions:

$$AUX_1 = \{Y_{t-i}, Y_{t-i}Y_{t-j}\} \quad \text{with } i,j = 1,\ldots p \tag{3.2}$$

$$AUX_2 = \{Y_{t-i}, Y_{t-i}Y_{t-j}, Y_{t-i}Y_{t-j}^k\} \quad \text{with } i,j = 1,\ldots,p;\ k = 2,3 \tag{3.3}$$

$$AUX_3 = \{Y_{t-i}, Y_{t-i}Y_{t-j}, Y_{t-j}^3\} \quad \text{with } i,j = 1,\ldots,p \tag{3.4}$$

The three corresponding test statistics are:[8] $S_1 \sim \chi^2_{(\frac{1}{2}p(p+1))}$, $S_2 \sim \chi^2_{(\frac{1}{2}p(p+1)+2p^2)}$, and $S_3 \sim \chi^2_{(\frac{1}{2}p(p+1)+p)}$. Finally, in the test for linearity against the bilinear model (Subba Rao and Gabr, 1984), the set of explanatory variables in the auxiliary regression is:

$$AUX_4 = \{Y_{t-i}\hat{\varepsilon}_{t-j}\} \quad \text{with } i = 1,\ldots,m;\ j = 1,\ldots,k \tag{3.5}$$

Under the null hypothesis of linearity, the corresponding $BL(p,m,k)$ statistic is asymptotically distributed as a χ^2_{mk}.

The results of the diagnostic and linearity tests for the residuals from the fitted autoregressive models, presented in table 3.2, indicate substantial evidence of non-linearity. The portmanteau statistic leads to rejection of the linearity null for all series but quarterly Exports and annual Consumption and Imports. The BDS test rejects linearity in all cases, with the only exception of quarterly exports. As for the linearity tests against specific alternatives, there is strong evidence of conditional heteroskedasticity, some support for threshold-type specifications, while little support for bilinear effects.[9]

Overall, this preliminary analysis enables us to confirm, for Italian macroeconomic data, the presence of significant neglected non-linearity. Such finding has been reported by many authors for a number of different countries and time periods (Mills, 1995; Brunner, 1992; Lee *et al.*, 1993). In the following sections we turn the evaluation of the hypotheses that cyclical asymmetries are an important feature of macro-dynamics, and that these asymmetries are sufficient to account for the finding of neglected non-linearity.

[8]The S_1 statistic can be shown to be asymptotically equivalent to the additivity test of Tsay (1986).

[9]It should be noted that the fact that the results of linearity tests are similar for the post-war series and for the historical series, rules out the possibility that the detection of non-linearities is actually due to the inappropriate treatment of outliers (war years).

3.3 Testing for Business Cycle Asymmetries

A large empirical literature on testing for business cycle asymmetries has developed in the last decade. One approach, originally proposed by Neftci (1984), was later followed in the empirical analyses of Falk (1986), Sichel (1989), and Rothman (1991). Neftci's testing procedure, based on a Markov chain representation of the cyclical process, considers the sample evidence on the signs of consecutive changes in a stationary process taken as an indicator of the state of the business cycle. The idea underlying the test is that the behaviour of a symmetric cyclical series would be similar during upswings and downswings, in the sense that the probabilities of transitions from one state would be equal to the probabilities of transitions from the other state. The test can be briefly described as follows. Let I_t be a procyclical stationary time series, and define the state indicator sequence by:

$$I_t = \left\{ \begin{array}{ll} 1 & \text{if } \Delta x_t > 0 \\ 0 & \text{if } \Delta x_t \leq 0 \end{array} \right\} \tag{3.6}$$

Assuming that the state indicator is stationary and that it can be represented by a first order Markov process[10], the likelihood function corresponding to a given realization is then given by:

$$L(S_t, p_{11}, p_{00}) = \pi_0 p_{11}^{n_{11}} (1 - p_{11})^{n_{12}} p_{22}^{n_{22}} (1 - p_{22})^{n_{21}} \tag{3.7}$$

where $p_{ij} = P(I_t = j | I_{t-1} = i)$ and n_{ij} is the number of occurrences of $(I_t = j\ I_{t-1} = i)$, with $j, i =$ 1, 2. Estimates of the transition probabilities are then obtained as count estimates:[11]

$$\hat{p}_{ij} = \frac{n_{ij}}{n_{i1} + n_{i2}} \tag{3.8}$$

The null hypothesis $H_0 : p_{11} = p_{22}$ is tested against the alternative $H_1 : p_{11} \neq p_{22}$. The test can be implemented by maximizing the log-likelihood

[10] The first order assumption is made here for simplicity of exposition, while Neftci's procedure also considers a second order Markov chain.

[11] One issue to be dealt with is the treatment of π_0, the probability of the initial state. This is generally either assumed to be equal to the ergodic probability vector, or ignored for simplicity (assuming that T is large enough, or that the process started at its stationary distribution, or on empirical grounds).

with and without the constraint. The likelihood ratio statistic (times −2) is asymptotically distributed as a χ^2 with 1 d.f. (see Anderson and Goodman, 1957).

A second approach to testing for BCA was proposed by DeLong and Summers (1986), who tested for asymmetry by examining skewness coefficients of cyclical components of economic time series. The idea underlying their testing procedure is that if recessions are brief and severe, while expansions are longer and more gradual, the median output growth rate should exceed the mean, and there should be significant (negative) skewness in a frequency distribution of growth rates of output. A test for steepness asymmetry can therefore be performed by using the standardized skewness coefficient (SK):[12]

$$SK = \frac{1}{T}\sum_t \left(\frac{y_t - \bar{y}}{\sigma_y}\right)^3 \tag{3.9}$$

Since the observations on the growth rates are serially correlated, the formula for the asymptotic standard error of the coefficient of skewness of an i.i.d. random variable is inapplicable. An asymptotic standard error for SK can be obtained either by means of Montecarlo simulations, following DeLong and Summers (1986), as in Sichel (1993), or computing the Newey and West (1987) asymptotic standard error (consistent in the presence of serial correlation):

$$ASE_{SK} = \sqrt{\frac{\hat{\sigma}_z^2}{T}\sum_{j=-m}^{m}\left(1 - \left|\frac{j}{m}\right|\right)\rho_z(j)} \tag{3.10}$$

where $z_t = \left(\frac{y-\bar{y}}{\sigma_y}\right)^3$, and $\rho_z(j)$ is the j-th autocorrelation of z_t. The sample mean of z_t, divided by the standard error in (3.10), is asymptotically normally distributed.

Table 3.3 presents the results obtained by applying Neftci-type and skewness tests to the set of Italian macroeconomic time series described in section 3.2. The Neftci-type tests are presented in three alternative versions: the first assumes a first order Markov process for the indicator function; the second

[12] Applying this procedure to annual and quarterly GNP and industrial production for the U.S. and five other OECD countries DeLong and Summers found little evidence of asymmetry for production series. They confirmed the findings of Neftci for quarterly U.S. unemployment series, but failed to do so for any of the other OECD countries.

assumes a second order process, and tests *partial* symmetry, in the sense that only the probability of observing an expansion conditional on having observed two consecutive expansions is tested for equality to its contraction counterpart; the third version assumes again a second order process, but tests the stronger restriction of complete symmetry, in the sense that *mixed* transition probabilities are also restricted to be equal under the null. The Neftci-type testing procedure provides estimates of the transition probabilities consistent with the hypothesis of steepness asymmetry (table 3.3). Such asymmetry, however, is not statistically significant for any of the series analysed. The results of the skewness tests also provide little support for the presence of asymmetries. Indeed, even the pattern of signs for the skewness statistics suggests little qualitative evidence of steepness-type asymmetry.

Overall, there seems to be little evidence of asymmetry. Some comments are in order, though: first, as argued in Neftci (1984) and Sichel (1989), these tests have low power in the presence of noise or measurement error. Second, the possible role of the level of aggregation should be considered: as it is argued in McNevin and Neftci (1992) and Rothman (1991), to the extent that the cyclical behaviour of industries is out of phase over the business cycle, an aggregate time series will be more symmetric than its components, even if the individual industries display significant asymmetries. Third, and more generally, the procedures applied by Neftci and DeLong and Summers are non-parametric tests that, being very general, have very low power.[13]

3.4 Modelling Business Cycle Asymmetries

Most of the literature on testing for BCA does not distinguish between the respective roles of the propagation mechanism and of the impulses (on these issues, see Potter, 1994). In this sense, non-parametric testing for BCA *per se* is not particularly informative, as it does not add much to our understanding of business cycle dynamics. Rather than just detecting the presence of asymmetries, it would be of interest to know, for example, whether economies respond

[13] For alternative approaches to testing for BCA see e.g. Stock (1987), Diebold and Rudebusch (1990), Hussey (1992), Brunner (1992), McQueen and Thorley (1993), Beaudry and Koop (1993), Acemoglu and Scott (1994).

differently to shocks over different phases of the business cycle; whether they respond in the same way to positive and negative shocks, which is a related, but different hypothesis; further, whether there are asymmetries in the dynamics governing the transitions from one phase to the other.

However, removing the linearity assumption opens the way to a potentially infinite number of approaches to non-linear time series modelling.[14] One particularly attractive approach to the departure from the linearity-symmetry assumption is the class of regime switching models. The essential idea of regime switching models is that some subsets of the data, in this case expansions and contractions, should be treated as different probabilistic objects. Two different approaches to regime switching are investigated in this work: threshold autoregressive and Markov-switching models.

In threshold autoregressive models, the state of the system is defined by the directly observable history of the time series, and regime changes are described as a deterministic function of past realizations of some observed variable. The overall process is non-linear, while following a linear AR model in each regime.[15] Within the class of TAR models, in this paper we consider the Self-Exciting Threshold Autoregressive (SETAR) model, which can formally be represented as follows:

$$y_t = \alpha_i + \phi_i(L)y_t + \varepsilon_{it} \qquad \text{if } y_{t-d} \in A_i \qquad \text{with } i = 1, ..., k \tag{3.11}$$

$$\text{where } \phi_i(L) = \phi_{1i}L + \phi_{2i}L^2 + ... + \phi_{pi}L^p \qquad \text{and } A_i = [r_{i-1}, r_i) \tag{3.12}$$

The economy is thus characterized by abrupt switches between k regimes, where the switching dynamics depend on the value taken by some observable variable, in general, or by the same variable being modelled in the case of SETAR models. This modelling approach was introduced in Tong (1983) and developed further in Tsay (1989) and Potter (1995).

[14]See Tong (1990) for a comprehensive introductory text.

[15]These models can have a number of attractive features, such as limit cycles, amplitude dependent frequencies, and jump phenomena. Also, modelling regime changes as a deterministic function of past realizations of some observed variable greatly simplifies estimation. However, TAR models have not been widely used in applications because it is to a large extent arbitrary how to identify the threshold variable and the associated threshold values.

Table 3.4 presents estimates for SETAR models applied to annual-long and quarterly-short Italian GDP. The optimal specification for each series was obtained by maximizing the AIC over a grid of threshold values (r), delay parameters (d) and autoregressive order (p).[16] Looking at the results for GDP, expansions and contractions are characterized as regimes of positive high and low (but positive) growth. The high-growth regime displays greater variability for both long-annual and short-quarterly data. The persistence of shocks, measured as the sum of the coefficients of the moving average representation of the estimated autoregressive model, is relatively higher for expansions (1.52) than for contractions (1.20) for short-quarterly data, while the opposite holds for long-annual data (1.03 and 1.56, respectively). A comparison of the last column of tables 3.1 and 3.4 shows a substantial improvement of fit relative to the linear autoregressive representation (R^2 increases from 0.47 to 0.54 and from 0.66 to 0.71 for the quarterly and annual series, respectively).

In the class of Markov-Switching (henceforth MS) models, the state of the economy is latent. The economy alternates between a finite number of states characterized by different sets of parameters, and discrete switches between the states are the outcomes of an unobservable state variable modelled as a Markov chain. In the original model proposed by Hamilton (1989), the first difference of real GNP is specified as a non-linear stationary process given by the sum of a state-dependent mean and an AR(4) process:

$$y_t = \alpha_0 + \alpha_1 s_t + z_t \tag{3.13}$$

where $\phi(L)z_t = \varepsilon_t$, and $\varepsilon_t \sim N(0, \sigma^2)$ i.i.d., independent of the switching mean at all leads and lags. The model can therefore be written as:

$$y_t - \mu_t = \phi_1(y_{t-1} - \mu_{t-1}) + ... + \phi_4(y_{t-4} - \mu_{t-4}) + \varepsilon_t \tag{3.14}$$

where $\mu_{s_t} = \alpha_0 + \alpha_1 s_t$. The unobservable state-variable is subject to discrete shifts between high-growth and low-growth states. The dynamics of these discrete shifts are described by a first-order Markov chain with constant

[16] We considered more appropriate to weigh the AIC for each of the two regimes by the respective number of observations, as opposed to no weighing (see e.g. Krager, 1992).

transition probabilities:

$$Q = \begin{bmatrix} p & 1-p \\ 1-q & q \end{bmatrix} \tag{3.15}$$

On the basis of an observed series, the objective is therefore to obtain simultaneously inference about the values taken at each point in time by the unobservable state, a description of the dynamics governing the transitions from one regime to the other, and estimates of the parameters characterizing the two regimes.[17]

Table 3.5 presents estimates for Markov-Switching models applied to annual-long and quarterly-short GDP.[18] Expansions and contractions are again characterized as regimes of high and low, but positive, growth. Interestingly, both long-annual and short-quarterly data offer a similar characterization of cyclical phases. The high-growth regime displays variability substantially higher than the low-growth regime, consistently with the finding reported by a number of authors that the main feature of contractions is higher volatility (e.g. French and Sichel, 1993). The measure of persistence of shocks is also systematically higher for contractions than for expansions, in contrast with the results obtained for the US economy, with a different methodology, by Beaudry and Koop (1993). The estimates for the transition probabilities are consistent with the presence of steepness asymmetry: expansions are more persistent, and thus have higher expected duration, than contractions. The improvement of fit relative to the linear autoregressive representation is even more pronounced than for the SETAR model: the last columns of tables 3.1 and 3.5 show that R^2 increases from 0.47 to 0.57 and from 0.66 to 0.74 for the quarterly and annual series, respectively).

---

[17]For the problems arising in making inference with MS models see e.g. Lamei (1990), Hansen (1992), Boldin (1992), Garcia and Perron (1996).

[18]It should be noted that the model we estimated is the one in Hamilton (1990), rather than the basic MS model, thus enabling estimation with the EM algorithm. This model, in which the parameters of the autoregressive representation - rather than the means - change with the unobserved state, has a more intuitive interpretation and is more directly comparable with the SETAR model, besides being computationally less demanding.

3.5 Do Business Cycle Asymmetries Account for Non-linearities?

As discussed in section 3.2, a number of authors have recently found evidence of neglected non-linearity in economic time series (see e.g. Lee *et al.*, 1993, Brock and Potter, 1993). This evidence suggests that the information contained in macroeconomic data is not fully extracted with the use of linear models. On the other hand, these studies generally fall short of providing either an explanation for the presence of neglected non-linearity, or explicit non-linear models to better exploit the information contained in macroeconomic data.

We suggest that business cycle asymmetries would provide an intuitive economic interpretation as well as a *parsimonious* representation of non-linearities in economic time series. We examine this conjecture by posing the following question can business cycle asymmetries account for the evidence of neglected non-linearity in economic time series? To this end, tables 3.6 and 3.7 display the results of diagnostic tests applied to the residuals from estimated SETAR and Markov-Switching models, respectively (these are to be compared with the results presented in table 3.2).

Looking at the test statistics for the residuals from SETAR models, the portmanteau statistics lead to accept the linearity null for all series but quarterly Consumption and Investment and annual Investment. The BDS test statistic, though, leads to rejection of linearity in almost all cases. The results for the residuals from the Markov-Switching models, however, are much more clear-cut in indicating little evidence of neglected non-linearity. For all quarterly series, with the only exception of private consumption, there is no evidence of neglected non-linearity. The results are less striking for annual-long series, but the linearity null is not rejected for Exports and GDP. Overall, the answer to our question is affirmative: allowing for two (business cycle) regimes is sufficient, for a large number of time series, to remove the evidence of neglected non-linearity.[19]

[19] One common criticism to the literature on non-linearities in economic time series is that rejecting linear representation against a particular alternative is not enough to justify models with non-linearity in mean. It should be noted that this criticism does not apply

3.6 Summary and Conclusions

This chapter has analyzed Italian macroeconomic data to investigate qualitative differences in the way an economy behaves at different stages of the business cycle. The existence of business cycle asymmetries, it has been argued, would have important implications for economic theory, econometric modelling, and policy-making. We applied various asymmetry and non-linearity tests to both annual post-unity and quarterly post-war time series. We then modelled the dynamics of recessions and expansions by means of threshold autoregressive and Markov-switching models.

The results of the analysis are mixed. On the one hand, consistently with the existing evidence for the US and the UK, we find that non-parametric tests provide relatively little support for asymmetries. On the other hand, quite interestingly, the paper shows that allowing for cyclical asymmetries can be sufficient to account for neglected non-linearities in Italian macroeconomic time series.

This is an important finding, since cyclical asymmetries would provide not only a parsimonious representation of non-linearities in economic time series, but also an intuitive economic interpretation. In particular, business cycle theories based on financial fragility predict cyclical asymmetries, due to the fact that the sensitivity of aggregate activity to shocks is higher when debt levels are high, and that debt levels, in turn, display significant cyclical fluctuations.

---

to the results of this section, as what is shown here is that simply allowing for a piece-wise linear representation in two separate (business cycle) regimes is sufficient to remove the presence of residual non-linearity.

Table 3.1: Descriptive statistics of raw series and residuals from AR models

	Original series				Residuals from autoregressive models						
	Mean	St.Dev.	Skew.	Kurt.	Skew.	Kurt.	Q1	Q2	Q3	Q4	R^2
Quarterly series											
GDP	0.95	1.20	0.79	6.14	1.08	8.15	0.91	0.95	0.99	0.84	0.47
Consumption	1.05	0.90	1.39	10.51	1.36	12.50	0.83	0.94	0.98	0.88	0.78
Investment	0.70	2.23	-0.04	3.35	0.32	4.01	0.89	0.99	0.96	0.93	0.27
Exports	1.68	3.31	-0.06	3.16	-0.06	3.14	1.00	0.98	0.84	0.90	0.44
Imports	1.61	3.36	-1.08	5.19	-0.69	3.85	0.98	0.88	0.79	0.26	0.49
Annual series											
GDP	1.51	2.47	0.05	2.59	1.22	15.13	0.94	0.99	0.99	0.95	0.66
Consumption	1.53	2.25	0.69	3.61	2.59	21.40	0.93	0.99	0.97	0.99	0.75
Investment	1.15	7.66	0.01	10.42	-0.88	9.09	0.93	0.89	0.36	0.46	0.31
Exports	2.19	7.56	-0.22	3.51	-1.30	19.49	0.95	0.99	0.99	0.99	0.68
Imports	1.92	7.42	-0.21	4.19	0.47	6.09	0.96	0.64	0.31	0.23	0.63

Note: the Q1 to Q4 columns report p-values for portmanteau test.

Table 3.2: Residual diagnostics and linearity tests

	McLeod-Li		BDS				ARCH		Bilinear		STAR		
	Q1	Q4	2	3	4	5	LM1	LM4	1,1	2,2	S1	S2	S3
Quarterly series													
GDP	0.02	0.17	0.00	0.02	0.08	0.02	0.02	0.03	0.64	0.37	0.80	0.02	0.15
Consumption	0.00	0.00	0.00	0.00	0.00	0.00	0.00	0.00	0.01	0.02	0.00	0.00	0.00
Investment	0.00	0.01	0.00	0.00	0.00	0.00	0.00	0.00	0.19	0.30	0.06	0.05	0.10
Exports	0.78	0.86	0.81	0.85	0.46	0.25	0.80	0.85	0.67	0.43	0.86	0.27	0.73
Imports	0.00	0.00	0.00	0.00	0.01	0.02	0.00	0.00	0.43	0.26	0.06	0.28	0.06
Annual series													
GDP	0.13	0.00	0.00	0.00	0.00	0.00	0.13	0.00	0.06	0.36	0.66	0.06	0.53
Consumption	0.88	0.43	0.00	0.00	0.00	0.00	0.88	0.44	0.13	0.03	0.05	0.01	0.10
Investment	0.03	0.03	0.00	0.00	0.00	0.00	0.03	0.01	0.15	0.03	0.00	0.00	0.00
Exports	0.00	0.00	0.01	0.00	0.00	0.00	0.00	0.00	0.45	0.19	0.02	0.08	0.03
Imports	0.20	0.74	0.00	0.00	0.00	0.00	0.20	0.71	0.93	0.23	0.35	0.15	0.25

Note: the figures reported are p-values; see section 3.2 for a description of the test statistics.

Table 3.3: Asymmetry tests

	Transition probabilities test					Skewness coefficient test			
	P11	*P22*	*CHI1*	*CHI2*	*CHI3*	*Sk.*	*S.E.*	*Sk/S.E.*	*SN*
Quarterly series									
GDP	0.39	0.33	0.45	0.69	0.34	0.79	0.79	1.01	0.84
Consumption	0.57	0.57	0.94	0.69	0.90	1.39	1.57	0.89	0.81
Investment	0.48	0.43	0.55	0.90	0.67	-0.04	0.44	-0.10	0.46
Exports	0.31	0.38	0.32	0.47	0.55	-0.06	0.24	-0.25	0.40
Imports	0.38	0.44	0.50	0.06	0.13	-1.08	0.75	-1.43	0.08
Annual series									
GDP	0.29	0.41	0.16	0.09	0.17	0.05	0.40	0.13	0.55
Consumption	0.47	0.51	0.65	0.24	0.07	0.69	0.65	1.06	0.86
Investment	0.38	0.44	0.44	0.05	0.14	0.01	1.29	0.01	0.50
Exports	0.42	0.35	0.44	0.46	0.61	-0.22	0.43	-0.50	0.31
Imports	0.37	0.41	0.58	0.88	0.72	-0.21	0.41	-0.50	0.31

Note: the figures reported for CHI and SN are p-values; see section 3.3 for a description of the test statistics.

Table 3.4: Estimates of SETAR regime switching models

	d,r	*c*	*b1*	*b2*	*b3*	*b4*	*mu*	*s2*	Pers.	N.Obs.	R^2
Quarterly GDP	y(t-3)<1.06	0.38	0.37	0.21	0.00	-0.24	0.79	0.57	1.52	81	0.54
		(.12)	(.1)	(.09)	(.08)	(.13)	.	.	.	.	
	y(t-3)>1.06	1.09	0.23	0.16	-0.02	-0.21	1.14	2.06	1.20	70	
		(.43)	(.13)	(.16)	(.17)	(.2)	.	.	.	.	
Annual GDP	y(t-2)<1.58	0.45	0.03	.	.	.	0.48	4.16	1.03	66	0.71
		(.27)	(.11)	.	.	.	.	.	.	.	
	y(t-2)>1.58	1.83	0.36	.	.	.	2.63	5.42	1.56	63	
		(.39)	(.12)	.	.	.	.	.	.	.	

Note: standard errors reported in parenthesis; d=delay, r=threshold, c=intercept, b=auto-regressive parameters, mu=mean, s2=variance, pers=measure of persistence. See section 3.4 for a description of the estimated model.

Table 3.5: Estimates of Markov-Switching models

	Regime	*c*	*b1*	*b2*	*b3*	*b4*	*s2*	*p*	*mu*	Pers.	R^2
Quarterly GDP	Low	0.54	0.48	0.10	-0.06	-0.18	0.63	0.90	0.86	1.50	0.57
		(.12)	(.09)	(.08)	(.07)	(.07)	(.09)	(.05)	.	.	
	High	-0.52	-0.31	0.24	0.48	1.56	0.91	0.47	1.47	7.86	
		(.5)	(.15)	(.19)	(.28)	(.36)	(.33)	(.18)	.	.	
Annual GDP	Low	1.19	-0.49	.	.	.	3.36	0.92	0.81	0.67	0.74
		(.47)	(.19)	.	.	.	(.58)	(.29)	.		
	High	0.57	0.76	.	.	.	2.85	0.90	2.38	4.07	
		(.22)	(.18)	.	.	.	(.47)	(.38)	.	.	

Note: standard errors reported in parenthesis; c=intercept, b=autoregressive parameters, mu=mean, s2=variance, p=transition probability, pers=measure of persistence. See section 3.4 for a description of the estimated model.

Table 3.6: Diagnostic statistics for residuals from SETAR models

	McLeod-Li				BDS			
	Q1	Q2	Q3	Q4	2	3	4	5
Quarterly series								
GDP	0.04	0.12	0.17	0.26	0.00	0.01	0.02	0.00
Consumption	0.01	0.02	0.04	0.08	0.00	0.00	0.00	0.00
Investment	0.00	0.00	0.00	0.00	0.00	0.00	0.00	0.00
Exports	0.86	0.77	0.90	0.96	0.84	0.77	0.96	0.59
Imports	0.27	0.51	0.50	0.67	0.02	0.13	0.22	0.68
Annual series								
GDP	0.43	0.26	0.41	0.34	0.16	0.09	0.06	0.15
Consumption	0.08	0.14	0.25	0.37	0.00	0.00	0.00	0.00
Investment	0.01	0.01	0.00	0.00	0.00	0.00	0.00	0.00
Exports	0.75	0.43	0.61	0.76	0.12	0.00	0.00	0.00
Imports	0.06	0.17	0.31	0.15	0.07	0.00	0.00	0.68

Note :figures reported for the test statistics are p-values; see section 3.2 for a description of the tests.

Table 3.7: Diagnostic statistics for residuals from Markov-Switching models

	McLeod-Li				BDS			
	Q1	Q2	Q3	Q4	2	3	4	5
Quarterly series								
GDP	0.24	0.32	0.41	0.58	0.59	0.49	0.36	0.61
Consumption	0.03	0.05	0.11	0.02	0.00	0.00	0.00	0.00
Investment	0.45	0.75	0.66	0.76	0.72	0.29	0.14	0.20
Exports	0.42	0.21	0.34	0.49	0.22	0.04	0.05	0.03
Imports	0.78	0.84	0.94	0.96	0.19	0.20	0.54	0.98
Annual series								
GDP	0.55	0.58	0.70	0.84	0.49	0.37	0.41	0.21
Consumption	0.07	0.10	0.00	0.00	0.20	0.02	0.00	0.00
Investment	0.00	0.00	0.00	0.00	0.00	0.00	0.00	0.00
Exports	0.88	0.98	0.88	0.94	0.63	0.99	0.71	0.61
Imports	0.01	0.04	0.07	0.10	0.01	0.01	0.00	0.00

Note: figures reported for the test statistics are p-values; see section 3.2 for a description of the tests.

Chapter 4

Distribution Dynamics of Corporate Financial Positions

4.1 Introduction

Mainstream business cycle theories generally abstract from the role of the financial system, while focusing on the role of various types of price rigidities or, more recently, agents' optimal responses to real exogenous shocks. In the past two decades, however, there has been an increasing interest in the links between the financial structure and aggregate activity. A number of authors have tried to formalize the idea that debt levels are not irrelevant, in the sense that the performance of agents, and of the aggregate economy, is not independent of the financial structure (Bernanke and Gertler, 1989; Greenwald and Stiglitz, 1993; Kiyotaki and Moore, 1997).[1] The central idea in this literature is that changes in agents' financial positions may significantly affect the behaviour of the economic system. In particular, the distribution of firms' balance sheet positions should be seen as one of the determinants of aggregate dynamics. This is so because, in the presence of informational asymmetries, net worth positions of borrowers determine their capacity to obtain external funds and, in turn, their investment and production levels.

Informational asymmetries play a major role in most business cycle models based on financial fragility. One implication of the presence of asymmetric

[1] Gertler (1988) and Bernanke (1993) provide surveys with a detailed account of historical developments.

information is that agents are qualitatively different from one another, to the extent that their financial positions differ. This implies that the representative agent framework becomes inadequate, since it is the heterogeneity of agents, with respect to their financial positions, which underlies financial fragility and is relevant for business cycle dynamics. Therefore, it is the evolving distribution of agents' financial positions, rather than aggregate indicators or disaggregate cross-sectional averages, that one should look at to learn about the changing financial structure of the economy and its interactions with aggregate activity.

Empirical studies of the cyclical dynamics of firms' financial positions have typically relied on either aggregate indicators (e.g. Eckstein and Sinai, 1986; Friedman, 1982) or cross-sectional averages for disaggregate data (e.g. Ciccolo, 1982; Seth, 1992). More recently, some authors have extended the analysis to specific classes of firms (e.g. the median, or the 90th percentile) in order to capture the dynamics of the relevant parts of the distribution (e.g. Bernanke and Campbell, 1988, 1990; Warshawsky, 1992). However, in a context of heterogeneous agents, it is more informative to study how the whole distribution of firms' financial structure evolves over time and interacts with aggregate fluctuations.

In this chapter we apply models of explicit distribution dynamics (Quah, 1994; 1996a) to study the evolution of the cross-section distribution of financial positions in a panel of US manufacturing firms. This enables us to obtain measures not only of the external-shape dynamics but also of the intra-distribution movements, and to study how these interact with aggregate activity.[2]

We find that the pattern of co-movements between aggregate economic activity and firms' financial positions is consistent with models where aggregate fluctuations are endogenously and jointly determined with financial conditions. This pattern is more pronounced in the upper tail of the distribution of firms' financial positions. The application of models of explicit distribution dynamics highlights substantial intra-distribution mobility, although there is only limited evidence of significant interactions between measures of intra-distribution dynamics and aggregate economic activity. Interestingly, though,

[2] This chapter is a revised version of Stanca *et al.* (1999).

we find evidence that movements of different parts of the leverage distribution contain important predictive information for aggregate investment growth. Finally, the internal dynamics of the distribution of firms' financial positions are more pronounced for small than for large firms, and display asymmetric patterns across business cycle phases.

The rest of the chapter is structured as follows. Section 4.2 briefly outlines the theoretical basis of the paper. Section 4.3 presents some basic facts, by looking at how summary statistics of the distribution of alternative indicators of firms' financial positions evolve over the business cycle. Section 4.4 models explicitly the evolving distribution of firms' financial positions, and considers its interactions with aggregate activity. Section 4.5 examines different patterns in the evolving distributions of small and large firms, and across business cycle phases. Section 4.6 summarizes the main results of the analysis.

4.2 Financial Factors and Aggregate Fluctuations

In the past two decades, a substantial body of literature has tried to refine the idea that debt levels are not irrelevant (in the Modigliani-Miller sense), so that the performance of firms, and of the aggregate economy, is not independent of the financial structure. In the modern literature on financial business cycles, it is possible to distinguish between two interpretations, characterised by different (although not mutually exclusive) methodological approaches: the first, and most influential, is the New Keynesian view based on the financial accelerator (e.g. Bernanke and Gertler, 1989; Greenwald and Stiglitz, 1993; Kiyotaki and Moore, 1997); the second can be referred to as the Financial Instability Hypothesis (e.g. Taylor and O'Connell, 1985; Franke and Semmler, 1989; Delli Gatti *et al.*, 1993).

The recent New Keynesian (NK) literature on the financial accelerator builds on the advances in the economics of asymmetric information, and highlights the interaction between firms' net worth and the dead-weight losses arising from asymmetric information. The basic idea is that if a negative shock reduces the net worth of firms, these find it more costly and difficult to raise external funds. As a consequence, their investment demand falls, worsening the effect of an initial negative shock. This literature predicts that changes in credit-market conditions may significantly affect the response of the economic system to exogenous shocks. Therefore, the higher firms' leverage, the higher the amplitude and persistence of fluctuations arising in response to shocks.

The recent literature on the Financial Instability Hypothesis (FIH) builds on the influential work on financial crises by Minsky (1982) and Kindleberger (1978). Aggregate fluctuations are seen as an intrinsic feature of modern economies, whose instability is due to the developments over time of the financial structure. During an expansion, borrowers and lenders expect future cash flows to justify increasing debt levels. As optimistic expectations are fulfilled, profits, asset prices and debt levels increase. Both banks and firms contribute to the increase in the aggregate leverage ratio. As the proportion of hedge units in the population of borrowers decreases, however, financial fragility increases. At the aggregate level, when cash flows do not validate debt any more, the network of financial relations may collapse, with a financial crises setting in. Financial instability is thus seen an endemic tendency of modern economies.

With respect to the methodology, the NK literature generally interprets business cycle dynamics within the Frisch-Slutsky framework: observed fluctuations are the outcome of random impulses perturbing a stable propagation mechanism. Within this framework, financial market imperfections have an impact on the *propagation mechanism*, contributing to the transmission and amplification of shocks. Financial factors are indicated as a likely candidate to explain how relatively small exogenous shocks can produce large fluctuations in output. The FIH literature generally assumes simple macroeconomic relations, without explicit microfoundations. The dynamics of financial variables and aggregate activity are jointly determined in a (possibly deterministic) dynamic system which makes explicit the interactions between the two. Financial instability thus provides an explanation for the *endogenous* arising of aggregate fluctuations.

The predictions of these (not mutually exclusive) methodological approaches, the New Keynesian financial accelerator and the Financial Instability Hypothesis, will be the guiding principles of the empirical analysis in the following sections.

4.3 The Cyclical Behaviour of Firms' Financial Positions

This section presents some basic facts about the evolution of the distribution of firms' financial positions over the business cycle. We focus on two indicators of financial positions: the debt-to-asset ratio, an indicator of *solvency*, and the ratio of interest expenses to cash flow, an indicator of *liquidity*.[3]

Our analysis is based on the published company accounts of 1541 U.S. manufacturing firms, between 1978 and 1996, drawn from the Datastream International data set. Data were only available for stock market quoted companies, and attention was restricted to firms whose main product was in manufacturing. The data for firms that had changed the date of their accounting year-end were adjusted at the source on a twelve-month basis. Firms with some data missing were excluded from the sample.

We created two samples of firms: a fixed (balanced) sample containing only continuously listed companies, i.e. companies for which data were available for each year from 1986 to 1995; and a fluctuating (unbalanced) sample, containing all firms for which data were available for at least two consecutive years from 1978 to 1996. While the fixed sample allows to focus on a homogeneous data set, the former allows to avoid survivorship bias and not to limit excessively the number of observations.

The focus of our analysis is on the behaviour of corporate leverage, which we measured with the debt-to-asset ratio. This is defined as Total Loan Capital (Datastream code [321]) over Total Capital Employed [322]. The sample-selection criteria described above resulted in a fluctuating sample containing 819 companies with a varying number of observations over the period 1978-96, and a fixed sample of 231 companies for the period 1986-1995. Our second indicator, the ratio of interest expenses to cash flow (operating income before

[3] Bernanke and Campbell (1990) refer to a *solvency problem* as a debt-asset ratio greater than unity, and to a *liquidity problem* as an interest expense to cash flow ratio greater than one (or negative).

depreciation), is defined as [153]/([735]*[322]), while Total Sales correspond to the Datastream Code [104].

Table 4.1 presents descriptive statistics for the debt-asset ratio. For each year, the table displays absolute and relative measures of central location (the mean and the median) and of dispersion (the standard deviation and the interquartile range). The second column reports the corresponding growth rate of GDP. A number of important features emerge from the table. First, the pattern of the descriptive statistics is very similar across the two samples (fixed and fluctuating). This is reassuring, as it indicates that using the full-sample (fluctuating) panel is not likely to introduce major distortions due to the time-inconsistent nature of the data. Therefore, in what follows, our discussion will focus essentially on the results for the fluctuating sample, unless major differences arise with respect to the fixed sample. Second, both the absolute (mean) and the relative (median) measures of central location decrease initially and then increase substantially over the 1982-1989 expansion. They then reach a peak in 1990, one year into the 1989-91 recession. Third, the absolute and relative measures of dispersion also follow a similar cyclical pattern, reaching a peak in 1990 and 1991, respectively. Fourth, if we focus on the relative statistics (median and interquartile range), a similar cyclical pattern can be observed also in the aftermath of the 1989-1991 recession: debt ratios decrease in the early years of the upturn, but then reverse their trend as the expansion gains momentum.

Overall, this informal description indicates two recurrent patterns in the cyclical behaviour of the distribution of firms debt-asset ratios: during an upturn, and until shortly after the peak, the representative firm becomes progressively more leveraged; at the same time, the whole distribution becomes more dispersed, so that a higher number of firms become financially *fragile*.

Table 4.2 shows the evolution of the same set of statistics for the interest expenses-to-cash flow ratio. Concentrating again on relative measures for the fluctuating sample, a pattern similar to the one for debt-asset ratios can be observed, although somewhat more erratic. Interest expenses (relative to cash flow) for the median firm in the sample decrease in the first half of the 1980s, to increase thereafter and reach a peak at 0.33 in 1990. The behaviour of the interquartile range is similar, reflecting the fact that (as shown below) the pattern just described becomes more and more pronounced as one moves towards the upper tail of the distribution.

Figure 4.1 plots the cyclical behaviour of the four descriptive statistics for the 1982-1995 period. Consider the behaviour of the median debt-asset ratio. During the 1982-1990 upturn, it decreases initially, to increase consistently until the peak. During the following downturn, it keeps increasing initially, only to reverse its trend and continue decreasing after the 1991 trough. It then appears to continue its anti-clockwise motion, entering a new phase in 1995.[4]

It is interesting to observe that the measures of dispersion follow a similar anti-clockwise oscillatory pattern. This indicates that the cyclical dynamics of the distribution of firms debt-asset ratios should not be thought as parallel shifts of the whole distribution. On the contrary, figure 4.1 suggests the possibility that there are systematic patterns in the cyclical behaviour of the external shape, in the whole distribution, or in both.

Overall, the conclusion from this preliminary data description is that the observed patterns of firms' financial positions over the business cycle are consistent with the predictions of models where aggregate fluctuations are endogenously and jointly determined with financial conditions. So far, however, our analysis, has to a large extent abstracted from cross-sectional heterogeneity, that is, the fact that firms with different financial positions may behave and evolve over time in different ways. The evidence presented so far referred to either cross-sectional averages, or to specific classes of firms within the distribution.

Such an approach is not completely informative. It would instead be desirable to have a more complete description of at least three aspects: first, the dynamics of the external shape of the entire distribution, that is, the evolution of the distribution for the whole leverage-range (not only, say, the median or the ninetieth percentile); second, intra-distribution mobility, that

[4]The anti-clockwise motion indeed characterizes the whole distribution (the same pattern can be observed for selected percentiles of the interest-to-cash flow ratio distribution). Furthermore, the cyclical movements of the solvency ratio are more pronounced as one moves toward the upper end of the distribution.

is, the movements of individual firms from any one part of the distribution to any other; third, the out of sample projections of the dynamics observed in sample. The methods to derive such information, and their application to our data set, are the subject of the next section.

4.4 The Evolving Distribution of Financial Positions

The question we address in this section is whether the distribution of firms' balance sheet positions as a whole (as opposed to the cross-section representative element) can influence, and in turn can be affected by, the dynamics of the aggregate economy. The underlying idea is that it is the entire distribution of balance sheet positions which identifies financial fragility, and is thus potentially relevant for understanding business cycle dynamics. We start by briefly outlining some methodological aspects of models of explicit distribution dynamics (for a more detailed description see Quah, 1996a, 1996b). We then present the results of tests of the dynamic relation between measures of external shape and intra-distribution mobility, and measures of aggregate activity.

Let F_t denote the time t sectional distribution of firms' financial positions. This distribution evolves over time both in the relative positions of different elements of the cross-section (i.e. intra-distributionally), and in its external shape. Both these dynamics can be represented by a stochastic kernel equation:

$$\forall\ A:\ f_t(A) = \int M_t(y, A) f_{t-1}(dy) \tag{4.1}$$

where y is any subset of the state space A, f_t is the probability measure corresponding to F_t, and M_t is a sequence of stochastic kernels. If the state space, and thus F_t, is discrete, then M_t is a Markov chain transition probability matrix.

In this section we will parametrize the dynamics of the evolving distribution by a pair M_t, Q_t, where M_t is an nxn fractile transition probability matrix, and Q_t is an n-element quantile set, i.e. a time-indexed sequence of n

disjoint intervals. These are constructed by fixing on the open interval (0,1) a set of $n-1$ equally-spaced probabilities. At each time period t, the set P determines on F_t a corresponding set of quantiles Q_t, where by definition $p_i = F_t(q_i(t))$. Each quantile-set pair Q_t,Q_{t+1} defines an nxn transition probability matrix of transitions from F_t to F_{t+1}. Together, M_t and Q_t represent a time-varying (non-stationary) evolving distribution. If M is instead assumed time-invariant, it can be estimated by appropriate averaging.

In the following, intra-distribution mobility will thus be characterized by the transition matrices M_t, while the dynamics of the external shape of the distribution will be characterized by the sequence of quantiles Q_t. We experimented with alternative numbers of states, and found a five-state discretization a reasonable compromise between descriptiveness and richness of the dynamics.[5] In economic terms, the discretized state-space can be thought of as analogous to the tripartition, introduced by Minsky, into hedge, speculative, and Ponzi units.

An estimate of the average five-state fractile transition probability matrix M is given in table 4.3. This matrix was obtained by averaging the observed one-year transitions over every two consecutive years from 1978-1979 to 1995-1996. The first column gives the total number of transitions with starting points in the corresponding state. The estimates indicate substantial (average) intra-distribution mobility, as reflected by the relatively low diagonal entries. Note also that there is greater mobility at the upper end of the distribution (we will return below to the dynamics of intra-distribution mobility).

When M defines an irreducible and aperiodic Markov chain, the process has a unique ergodic distribution, which is approached at a geometric rate given by M's second largest eigenvalue. The ergodic distribution then provides an indication of the out-of-sample dynamics for the external shape implied by the observed pattern of intra-distribution mobility. However, (M, Q) implies such limiting behaviour only if Q is time invariant. We thus examine the observed dynamic behaviour of the quantile set, and will return to the out-of-sample external shape dynamics in section 4.5. In particular, the question

[5]Section 5 will show how the arbitrary discretization of the state-space can be integrated and checked for robustness by modelling the dynamics of the distribution with a continuous-state-space stochastic kernel.

we turn to is whether there is any statistically significant interaction between aggregate activity and our measures of the dynamics of the external shape of the distribution and, if so, in what direction.

Table 4.4 presents marginal significance levels for exclusion restrictions (Granger causality) tests in bivariate VARs including GDP growth and each of the quantiles q_t. For each lag-length (from 2 to 4), the first entry is the significance level for excluding the quantile displayed on the corresponding row in the equation for GDP growth; while the second entry is the significance level for the exclusion of GDP growth from the quantile equation. The test-statistics are not significant in virtually all cases, with the only exception of the uppermost quantile (i.e. the maximum) in the equation for GDP, at lag-length four. Overall, thus, there is no evidence of significant interactions between GDP growth and the dynamics of different parts of the distribution.

Consider now table 4.5, which presents in a similar way marginal significance levels for exclusion restriction tests in bivariate VARs including each of the quantiles q_t and, this time, Real Gross Private Investment growth. The results are striking in that individual quantiles display significant predictive power for investment growth, after taking into account lagged values of investment growth. This result holds for regressions with both lag-length 3 and 4, and is more evident for the middle range of the leverage distribution (i.e. quantiles 0.4 and 0.6). Interestingly, the additional predictive power does not apply in the opposite direction, that is, exclusion restrictions for lagged values of investment growth in equations for distribution quantiles cannot be rejected.[6]

Taken together, the figures in tables 4.4 and 4.5 suggest not only that there are significant interactions between the distribution of firms financial positions and aggregate economic activity, but also that these interactions are not simply a reflection of endogenous movements of firms' balance sheet positions in response to business cycle fluctuations. The evidence, although limited, suggests a causal direction (in the predictive sense) going from the evolving distribution of firms' net worth to aggregate performance.[7]

---

[6]It should not be overlooked, however, that the reliability of these test is limited, due to the small number of observations available.

[7]The results reported above were also found to be robust to the inclusion in the fore-

Let us now turn to the dynamics of intra-distribution mobility. In a context of asymmetric information, it has been shown that composition effects may play a role in explaining economic fluctuations That is, the repositioning of firms within the distribution of financial positions may by itself affect aggregate activity. This can be explained essentially by the fact that agency costs are a non-linear (convex) function of firms leverage positions (Greenwald and Stiglitz, 1993).

In our setting, information on the mobility between different parts of the distribution, for given external shape (quantile) dynamics, is contained in the transition matrices M_t. The degree of mobility, at each point in time, can be measured by calculating appropriate mobility indices from the time-varying transition matrices, as described in Quah (1996a). We will use three alternative indices, which can be calculated as follows:

$$\mu_1(t) = \frac{n - tr(M(t))}{n-1} \tag{4.2}$$

$$\mu_2(t) = \frac{n - \sum_j |\lambda_j(t)|}{n-1} \tag{4.3}$$

$$\mu_3(t) = 1 - |\lambda_2(t)| \tag{4.4}$$

where λ_j is the j-th largest eigenvalue of the estimated transition probability matrix.

The indices take value between 0 (maximum persistence) and 1 (maximum mobility). The three mobility indices are strongly and positively correlated with each other, and show substantial fluctuations, which appear particularly pronounced at the beginning of the sample, and tend to be negatively correlated with GDP growth. Table 4.6 presents significance levels of exclusion restrictions, and contemporaneous correlations, between mobility indices and investment growth, as described above for the analysis of quantiles dynamics.

casting equations of aggregate GDP (capturing the role of expected profitability), and to the inclusion of an aggregate leverage variable (so that the distributional dynamics could be distinguished from the aggregate dynamics). Neither experiment affected substantially the results of the Granger causality tests and, in particular, the significance of the additional predictive power for aggregate investment of individual quantiles of the debt-asset distribution.

The contemporaneous correlations suggest that intra-distribution mobility is weakly related to aggregate investment growth. The causality tests are not significant in most cases, with the exception of the equation for the first mobility index at lag 4, indicating that investment growth has some predictive power for intra-distribution mobility, but not vice versa. Overall, there seems to be little evidence that compositional effects may have a role in amplifying and propagating aggregate fluctuations.

4.5 Sectional and Time Heterogeneity

Empirical tests of financial business cycle theories generally rely on firms' cross-sectional heterogeneity. That is, the behaviour of firms is expected to differ depending on the extent to which finance constraints are binding. Most existing evidence on this issue can be traced back to the original work of Fazzari *et al.* (1988), who identified credit constrained firms on the basis of dividend pay-out behaviour, and showed that cash flows are more important for firms where internal funds are in short supply. More recently, Gertler and Gilchrist (1994) and Bernanke *et al.* (1996) found evidence supporting the hypothesis that, at the onset of a recession, credit-constrained firms reduce spending and production earlier and more sharply than firms with greater access to credit markets. In their study, firm-size was used as a proxy for credit market access, under the assumption that small firms are more likely to be subject to credit constraints.

We thus turn to the following question: how different are the cyclical dynamics of small and large firms? To address this question, we ordered our sample of firms on the basis of 1991 total assets, and split the sample into three groups with equal number of observations. Figure 4.2 compares the average growth rates of total sales for small (dotted line) and large firms (dashed line), while the full-sample (solid line) growth rate is reported for comparison. The figure shows that the cyclical fluctuations of total manufacturing sales are driven by small firms. That is, the growth rate for small firms exceeds the one for large firms when total manufacturing growth is increasing, while the opposite holds in the descending phase. Note also that the size-spread is more pronounced around turning points. The observed pattern thus confirms the findings in Bernanke *et al.* (1996): small firms, which are likely to be relatively more credit constrained, account for a relatively large part of aggregate cyclical volatility.

The next aspect we consider is the extent to which the distribution dynamics of financial positions differ between small and large firms. Figures 4.3 and 4.4 display stochastic kernels and the corresponding contour plots of the debt-to-asset ratio distribution for the small and large-firm sub-samples, respectively. These were estimated over 1-year transitions, and can be interpreted as the continuous state-space analogues of transition probability matrices.[8] For the large-firm sub-sample the ridge of the kernel is very pronounced, along the 45-degree diagonal, indicating significant persistence. On the other hand, the kernel for the small-firm sub-sample is much more dispersed around the 45-degree diagonal, showing substantial intra-distribution mobility. This asymmetry is particularly evident as one moves towards the upper end of the distribution: highly leveraged small firms are much more likely to increase their financial exposure or *reliquefy* than highly leveraged large firms.

The transitional dynamics described above were estimated by averaging over the time dimension, thus obscuring possible asymmetric patterns across business cycle phases. In fact, one of the implications of business cycle theories based on financial fragility is the presence of non-linearities in the response of the economy to external shocks. In particular, one should expect to observe business cycle asymmetries, due to the fact that the sensitivity of aggregate activity to shocks is higher when debt levels are high, and that debt levels, in turn, display significant cyclical fluctuations. In the New Keynesian literature this has led to the conclusion that the response to shocks should be greater during recessions, as emphasized in Bernanke *et al.* (1996).

This prediction has found some empirical support. Gertler and Hubbard (1988) re-estimated the Fazzari *et al.* (1988) investment-cash-flow equations, allowing liquidity effects to be different in recession years. Their results show

[8] Estimation of the transitional dynamics on a continuous state-space allows an indirect check of whether the (arbitrary) selection of the number of states in the discretization introduces substantial distortions. The stochastic kernels displayed in figures 3 and 4 have features which correspond closely to the five-state transition probability matrices.

that there is an asymmetric effect of internal net worth on investment, in the sense that cash flow effects for high-retention firms are substantially stronger in recession years. Kashhyap *et al.* (1994) examined the cyclical behaviour of U.S. manufacturing inventories, and found that financial constraints are binding during tight-money recessionary episodes, whereas there is little evidence of inventories being sensitive to financial factors out of these episodes.

To shed some light on the prediction of business cycle asymmetries, we turn to a slightly different but related question: how does the distribution of firms financial positions evolve during expansions and contractions? Figures 4.5 and 4.6 show stochastic kernels and contour plots of the debt-to-asset ratio distribution for contraction and expansion years, respectively. The plots indicate that at the lower end of the debt-asset ratio distribution (low leverage) the transitional dynamics are similar across cyclical phases, in that there is a similar tendency to move towards the middle of the distribution. The upper part of the distribution, however, displays a cyclical asymmetry, in that highly leveraged firms tend to reliquefy during contractions, while they display much more persistence during expansions.[9]

4.6 Summary and Conclusions

This chapter has considered the evidence on some implications of agents' heterogeneity for theories of macroeconomic fluctuations based on the role of financial variables. We modelled explicitly the distribution dynamics of financial positions in a panel of US manufacturing firms. This allowed us to obtain measures of both external-shape dynamics and intra-distribution mobility, and to study how these interact with aggregate activity.

We find a pattern of co-movements between aggregate economic activity and firms' financial positions which is consistent with models where aggregate fluctuations are endogenously and jointly determined with financial conditions. The application of models of explicit distribution dynamics reveals significant intra-distribution mobility, although there is only limited evidence

[9] These distribution dynamics seem to be consistent, although to a different degree for different parts of the distribution, with the phases of the credit cycle as described in Eckstein and Sinai (1986).

of significant interactions between measures of intra-distribution dynamics and aggregate economic activity. On the other hand, we find evidence that movements of different parts of the leverage distribution contain important predictive information for aggregate investment growth. The internal dynamics of the distribution of firms' financial positions are more pronounced for small than for large firms, and display asymmetric patterns across business cycle phases.

Although our results are not intended as formal tests of specific models, they take a first step towards taking into account agents' heterogeneity in the empirical study of aggregate dynamics, and provide important preliminary indications for theories of the business cycle based on the role of financial variables.

Table 4.1: Debt-Asset ratio (1980-1996)

		Fixed sample					Fluctuating sample				
Year	GDP g.r.	Mean	St.Dev.	Median	Int.Q.R.	N. of firms	Mean	St.Dev.	Median	Int.Q.R.	N. of firms
1980	-0.49	0.23	0.21	0.18	0.25	22	0.25	0.21	0.22	0.20	36
1981	1.59	0.22	0.25	0.13	0.26	36	0.21	0.21	0.14	0.21	56
1982	-1.84	0.29	0.25	0.28	0.41	66	0.28	0.23	0.26	0.34	90
1983	3.62	0.30	0.31	0.20	0.33	103	0.27	0.29	0.18	0.31	133
1984	5.63	0.29	0.27	0.25	0.30	132	0.28	0.25	0.25	0.30	165
1985	3.42	0.30	0.23	0.27	0.39	174	0.29	0.22	0.24	0.37	214
1986	2.88	0.33	0.27	0.27	0.41	231	0.32	0.26	0.25	0.38	274
1987	2.65	0.31	0.23	0.28	0.33	231	0.31	0.24	0.26	0.33	325
1988	3.54	0.31	0.22	0.28	0.32	231	0.32	0.24	0.28	0.33	356
1989	3.08	0.32	0.23	0.30	0.35	231	0.35	0.27	0.30	0.38	390
1990	1.25	0.35	0.32	0.31	0.34	231	0.37	0.32	0.31	0.38	437
1991	-1.07	0.32	0.29	0.27	0.35	231	0.35	0.31	0.29	0.40	496
1992	2.64	0.30	0.25	0.27	0.32	231	0.33	0.31	0.27	0.39	580
1993	2.30	0.29	0.25	0.24	0.31	231	0.29	0.28	0.22	0.35	663
1994	3.57	0.29	0.24	0.26	0.33	231	0.28	0.26	0.23	0.34	741
1995	2.28	0.28	0.23	0.23	0.34	231	0.28	0.26	0.23	0.38	743
1996	2.88	0.25	0.22	0.22	0.32	104	0.26	0.24	0.20	0.36	299
Average	2.23	0.29	0.25	0.24	0.34	173	0.30	0.26	0.25	0.34	353

Note: the fixed sample contains companies for which data were available for each year from 1985 to 1995; the fluctuating sample contains firms for which data were available for at least two consecutive years from 1978 to 1996; the second column reports, for reference, the growth rate of GDP.

Table 4.2: Interest-Cash flow ratio (1980-1996)

		Fixed sample					Fluctuating sample				
Year	GDP g.r.	Mean	St.Dev.	Median	Int.Q.R.	N. of firms	Mean	St.Dev.	Median	Int.Q.R.	N. of firms
1980	-0.49	0.38	0.55	0.23	0.25	14	2.75	11.43	0.26	0.32	27
1981	1.59	0.30	0.41	0.13	0.35	21	1.46	6.34	0.17	0.37	36
1982	-1.84	0.41	0.55	0.17	0.42	39	1.40	6.43	0.15	0.51	55
1983	3.62	0.30	0.38	0.14	0.33	65	0.59	2.89	0.13	0.36	83
1984	5.63	0.41	0.93	0.19	0.44	89	0.55	2.00	0.19	0.41	113
1985	3.42	0.40	0.65	0.26	0.41	125	0.88	4.30	0.25	0.42	159
1986	2.88	0.42	0.78	0.23	0.39	165	0.57	2.40	0.23	0.40	213
1987	2.65	0.35	0.64	0.19	0.36	165	0.37	0.63	0.18	0.39	253
1988	3.54	0.34	0.47	0.16	0.37	165	0.41	0.75	0.16	0.39	281
1989	3.08	0.56	1.94	0.19	0.43	165	0.85	2.66	0.19	0.47	313
1990	1.25	0.39	0.67	0.21	0.41	165	0.55	1.23	0.22	0.48	349
1991	-1.07	0.36	0.47	0.21	0.38	165	0.50	0.94	0.23	0.46	413
1992	2.64	0.33	0.55	0.16	0.33	165	0.40	0.73	0.18	0.39	481
1993	2.30	0.31	0.86	0.14	0.24	165	0.36	0.83	0.15	0.30	562
1994	3.57	0.21	0.30	0.12	0.24	165	0.30	0.84	0.14	0.29	627
1995	2.28	0.19	0.25	0.12	0.21	165	0.40	1.40	0.14	0.33	616
1996	2.88	0.18	0.28	0.08	0.22	73	0.37	0.95	0.12	0.30	252
Average	2.23	0.35	0.62	0.18	0.33	111	1.13	3.78	0.17	0.37	255

Note: the fixed sample contains companies for which data were available for each year from 1986 to 1995; the fluctuating sample contains firms for which data were available for at least two consecutive years from 1978 to 1996; the second column reports, for reference,the growth rate of GDP.

Table 4.3: Debt-Asset ratio (1978-96), transition probability matrix

# starting points	Quantile				
Year	0.2	0.4	0.6	0.8	1
(1039)	0.69	0.17	0.08	0.04	0.03
(1051)	0.22	0.50	0.18	0.07	0.03
(1042)	0.05	0.23	0.47	0.19	0.06
(1045)	0.04	0.06	0.22	0.52	0.16
(1038)	0.05	0.06	0.09	0.20	0.60

Note: transition probabilities were estimated by averaging the observed one-year transitions over every two consecutive years from 1978-1979 to 1995-1996. The first column reports the number of firm/year pairs beginning in a given quantile.

Table 4.4: Debt-asset ratio: Quantiles-GDP growth (exclusion restrictions)

	Lag length						
Quantile	2		3		4		Cont. Corr.
(.2)	0.35	0.83	0.46	0.82	0.42	0.74	0.40
(.4)	0.43	0.59	0.55	0.50	0.63	0.37	0.42
(.6)	0.43	0.30	0.55	0.12	0.58	0.30	0.08
(.8)	0.37	0.30	0.56	0.47	0.70	0.78	0.09
(1)	0.64	0.53	0.34	0.44	0.01	0.48	-0.09

Note: the figures reported are p-values. For each lag-length, the first entry refers to the exclusion of the given quantile in the equation for GDP growth; the second entry refers to the exclusion of GDP growth in the equation for the given quantile. All VARs include a constant and were estimated using data from 1978 to 1996.

Table 4.5: Debt-asset ratio: Quantiles-Investment (exclusion restrictions)

	Lag length						
Quantile	2		3		4		Cont.Corr.
(.2)	0.41	0.80	0.10	0.74	0.01	0.60	-0.26
(.4)	0.85	0.72	0.05	0.61	0.00	0.72	-0.24
(.6)	0.89	0.94	0.01	0.22	0.00	0.57	-0.26
(.8)	1.00	0.96	0.11	0.85	0.10	0.30	-0.22
(1)	0.95	0.35	0.60	0.45	0.51	0.63	0.19

Note: the figures reported are p-values. For each lag-length, the first entry refers to the exclusion of the given quantile in the equation for Investment growth; the second entry refers to the exclusion of Investment growth in the equation for the given quantile. All VARs include a constant and were estimated using data from 1978 to 1996.

Table 4.6: Debt-asset ratio: Mobility-Investment (exclusion restrictions)

	Lag length						
Mob. Ind	2		3		4		Correl.
1	0.33	0.59	0.34	0.10	0.12	0.02	-0.09
2	0.59	0.24	0.64	0.06	0.22	0.06	0.15
3	0.51	0.60	0.45	0.47	0.15	0.34	0.19

Note: the figures reported are p-values. For each lag-length, the first entry refers to the exclusion of the given quantile in the equation for Investment growth; the second entry refers to the exclusion of Investment growth in the equation for the given mobility index. All VARs include a constant and were estimated using data from 1978 to 1996.

Figure 4.1: Debt-asset ratio distribution (1982-95): selected statistics

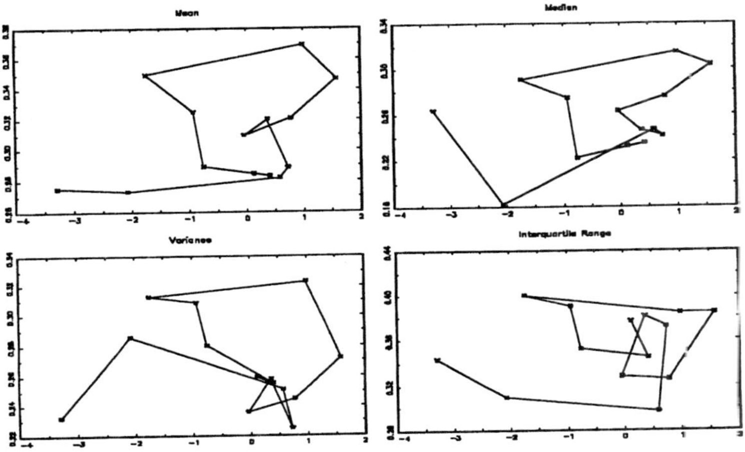

Figure 4.2: Growth rate of total sales: small and large firms

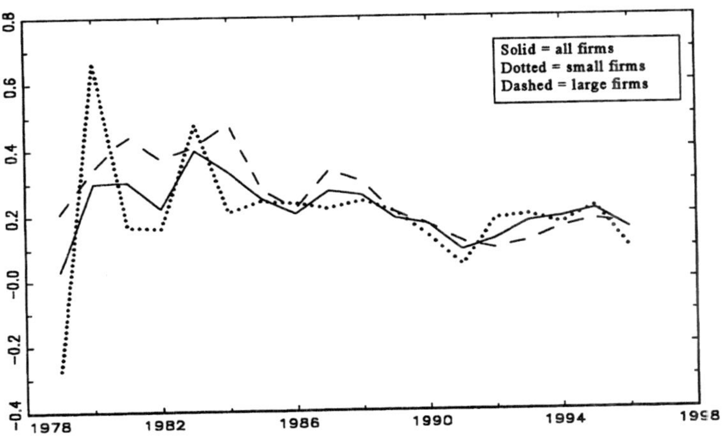

Figure 4.3: Debt-asset ratio, stochastic kernel (k=1): Large firms

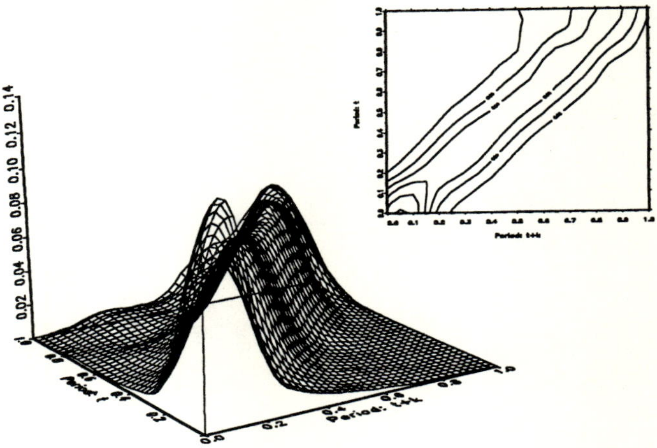

Figure 4.4: Debt-asset ratio, stochastic kernel (k=1): Small firms

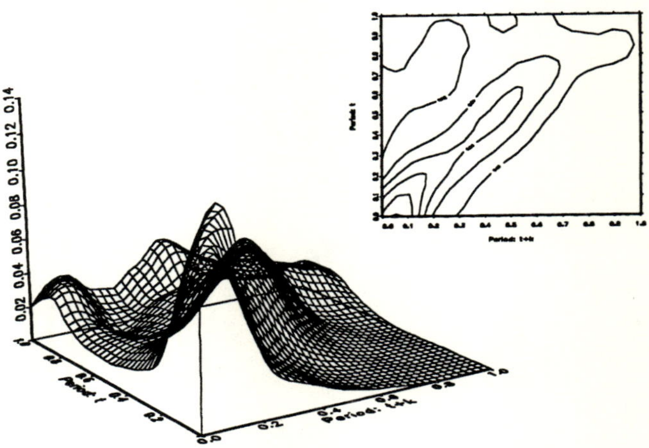

Figure 4.5: Debt-asset ratio, stochastic kernel (k=1): Contractions

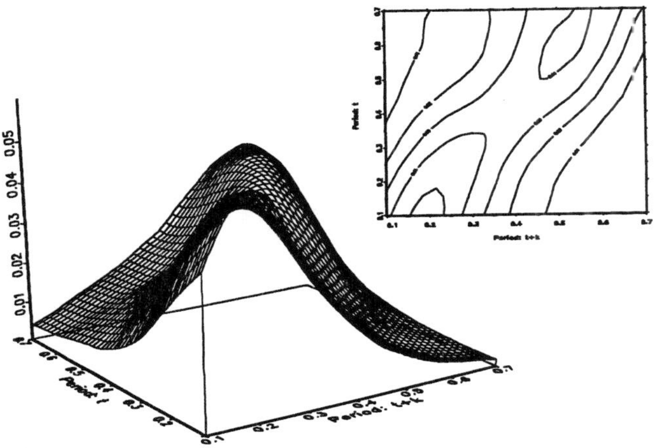

Figure 4.6: Debt-asset ratio, stochastic kernel (k=1): Expansions

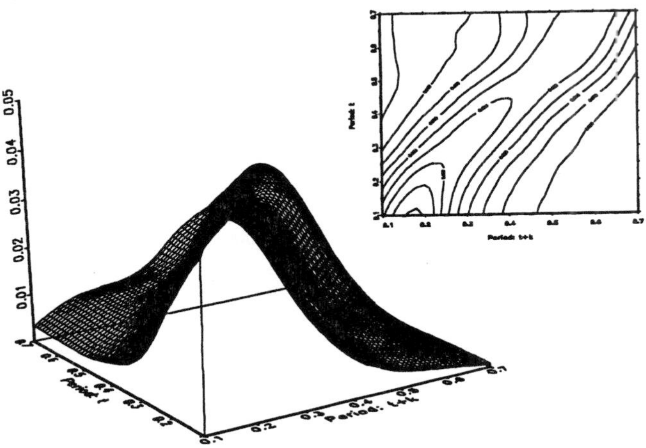

Chapter 5

Corporate Financial Positions and Investment Dynamics

5.1 Introduction

A number of recent papers have formalized the idea that changes in agents' financial conditions may contribute to amplify and propagate the impact of exogenous shocks on economic activity (see e.g. Bernanke and Gertler, 1989; Greenwald and Stiglitz, 1993; Kiyotaki and Moore, 1997). Asymmetric information in capital markets makes it costly for lenders to evaluate the quality of firms' investment projects, so that the cost of new debt or equity can be substantially higher than the opportunity cost of internal finance. As a consequence, for certain classes of firms investment depends on financial factors such as the availability of internal finance and the access to new debt or equity finance. This implies that when an adverse shock, real or monetary, worsens firms financial conditions, this negatively affects their internal finance and access to credit. At the macroeconomic level, the resulting decline in investment can thus amplify the cyclical downswing, through the so-called financial accelerator effect.[1]

One of the key elements of these financial business cycle theories is the existence of a two-way dynamic interaction between firms' investment decisions and their financial positions: over time financial conditions are affected by, and in turn affect, investment fluctuations. Existing empirical tests of such

[1]See Hubbard (1998) and Schiantarelli (1997) for recent comprehensive surveys.

theories, however, generally focus on the sensitivity of investment to financial factors within static (Gertler and Hubbard, 1988; Hayashi and Inoue, 1991; Hoshi *et al.*, 1991; Oliner and Rudebush, 1992; Hubbard *et al.*, 1995) or partially dynamic specifications (Fazzari *et al.*, 1988; Devereux and Schiantarelli, 1990; Blundell *et al.*, 1992; Whited, 1992; Bond and Meghir, 1994). Relatively little evidence is available about the time series interactions between a firm's financial condition and its investment decisions.

The objective of this chapter is to present some evidence from company account data on the dynamic relationship between firms' financial conditions and investment decisions. Our analysis contributes to the existing empirical tests of financial business cycle theories in three respects. First, by estimating vector autoregressive representations on panel data, we take explicitly into account the dynamic nature of the interaction between financial conditions and investment. Second, we examine some of the predictions of financial business cycle theories concerning time and sectional heterogeneity (Bernanke *et al.*, 1996; Gertler and Hubbard, 1988; Gertler and Gilchrist, 1994; Kashyap *et al.*, 1994). Third, we check the robustness of the results to the use of alternative indicators of financial conditions.[2]

The results of our empirical analysis complement and qualify earlier findings supporting the hypothesis that capital market imperfections have an important role in explaining investment spending. We also find significant evidence of both cross-sectional and time heterogeneity. On the one hand, the role played by financial factors is significantly more important for highly leveraged than for low debt firms. On the other hand, capital market frictions are shown to have asymmetric effects, displaying a larger impact in contractions than in expansions. This latter finding suggests a natural way to interpret the recent empirical literature documenting the presence of various types of asymmetries in aggregate economic fluctuations (see e.g. Sichel, 1993; Thoma, 1994; Potter, 1995)

The chapter is structured as follows. Section 5.2 provides the theoretical background, discussing the role of financial factors in aggregate fluctuations, and focusing on the recent financial business cycle theories based on infor-

[2] This chapter is a revised version of Stanca and Gallegati (1999).

mational asymmetries. Section 5.3 briefly reviews alternative approaches to empirical investment modelling. Section 5.4 provides the empirical motivation of the paper, considering the existing evidence on the role of financial factors for investment decisions, and discussing some limitations of the specifications adopted. Section 5.5 describes the econometric methodology and the data set, while section 5.6 presents the results of the empirical analysis. Section 5.7 concludes with the main implications and some suggestions for future research.

5.2 The Financial Propagation Mechanism

Traditional theoretical analyses of the determinants of investment typically abstract from financial considerations. This reflects to a large extent the influence of the work by Modigliani and Miller (1958), which provided a theoretical basis for the argument that real decisions of firms are separable from their financial structure. More precisely, their work demonstrated that, with perfect capital markets, no taxes or transaction costs, and with symmetric information, a firm's financial structure does not affect its market value. Therefore, under such conditions, the cost of internal and external funds is the same, and investment decisions are not affected by how they are financed (retained earnings, equity, or debt). This view has led most subsequent research on investment to focus on real factors, while typically disregarding the role of firms' financial positions and their access to credit.

The assumption that the investment decisions of firms are independent of financial factors has been gradually challenged by both theoretical and empirical studies. Stiglitz and Weiss (1981) and Myers and Majluf (1984) showed that the costs of internal and external finance may differ under more realistic assumptions about capital markets imperfections (e.g. transaction costs, tax advantages, agency problems, costs of financial distress, asymmetric information). More recently, the economics of asymmetric information has provided solid microeconomic foundations for the role of financial positions in determining investment decisions.

The central idea in this literature is that changes in agents' financial positions may significantly affect the behaviour of the economic system. This is so because, in the presence of informational asymmetries, net worth positions of borrowers determine their capacity to obtain external funds and, in turn, their investment and production levels. When, for example, a negative shock reduces the net worth of firms, these find it more costly and difficult to raise external funds. As a consequence, their investment demand falls, thus worsening the effect of an initial negative shock. Different aspects of this financial propagation mechanism have been emphasized in the recent works of Bernanke and Gertler (1989), Greenwald and Stiglitz (1993), and Kiyotaki and Moore (1997).[3]

Bernanke and Gertler (1989) focus on ex-post informational asymmetries. Highly indebted borrowers are more likely to be unable to repay their debts, which determines costly monitoring by the lender. A real or monetary adverse exogenous shock lowers current cash flows, thus reducing the ability of firms to finance investment projects internally and raising the cost of investment. The fall in investment spending lowers economic activity and cash flows in subsequent periods, propagating the initial shock. Greenwald and Stiglitz (1993) focus on ex-ante informational asymmetries. Firms require external funds to finance the wage bill, as there is a one-period lag between the use of variable inputs and the production of output. Since the access to external funds depends on the firm's balance sheet position, there is a tight connection between the firms' net worth and production. Kiyotaki and Moore (1997) develop a dynamic equilibrium model in which endogenous fluctuations in asset prices are the source of changes in net worth, access to credit, and spending. The key assumption is that lenders cannot force borrowers to repay debts unless the debts are secured, so that borrowers' assets serve both as factors of production and as collateral for new loans. When a shock lowers the value of the existing collateral, borrowing constraints become tighter and spending is reduced. The fall in spending in turn lowers the value of existing assets, causing further reductions in borrowing and spending.

These recent financial business cycle models have in common the prediction that the availability of finance is likely to have an effect on the investment

[3] Other important theoretical works on the financial propagation mechanism include Calomiris and Hubbard (1990) and Gertler (1992).

decisions of firms that face asymmetric information in capital markets. More precisely, the availability of internal funds allows firms to undertake investment projects without resorting to high-cost external finance. In addition, stronger balance sheet positions lower the cost of external finance. This result, it should be noted, is independent of how the real side of the investment decision is modelled. Regardless of the real determinants of investment demand, the supply of low-cost finance should enter the reduced form investment equation of firms for which internal and external finance are not perfect substitutes.

5.3 Empirical Investment Models

In the basic neoclassical model, investment is determined when the marginal cost of capital equals the marginal product of capital. Given technology, the optimal capital stock can be derived, and investment occurs to fill the gap between the optimal and the current capital stock. Under certain simplifying assumptions the demand for capital can be expressed as a function of the user cost of capital alone. Formally, the model can be derived from firms' maximization of profit (see Cho, 1996):

$$V_t = \sum_{j=0}^{\infty} \beta_{t+j} \left[p_{t+j} F\left(K_{t+j}, L_{t+j}\right) - w_{t+j} L_{t+j} - p^I_{t+j} I_{t+j} \right] \tag{5.1}$$

subject to

$$K_{t+j} = \left(1 - \delta\right) K_{t+j-1} + I_{t+j} \tag{5.2}$$

where β is the discount rate, p is the price of output, K is the capital stock, L is the labour input, w is the wage rate, I is gross investment, and p^I the price of investment goods. The first order conditions (F.O.C.s) for the capital stock imply that

$$\left(\frac{\partial F}{\partial K}\right)_t \simeq \frac{p^I_t}{p_t} \left(r_{t+1} + \delta - \pi^I_{t+1}\right) = J_t \tag{5.3}$$

Intuitively, at the optimum capital stock, the marginal product of capital equals the cost of using an additional unit of capital (the *user cost* of capital).

If the production function is CES:

$$Y_t = [\alpha K^\rho + (1-\alpha) L^\rho]^{\frac{1}{\rho}} \tag{5.4}$$

then

$$F_K = \alpha Y^{(1-\rho)} K^{(\rho-1)} \tag{5.5}$$

so the F.O.C. gives

$$K_t^* = \alpha^{\frac{1}{1-\rho}} Y_t J_t^{-\sigma} = A Y_t J_t^{-\sigma} \tag{5.6}$$

where σ is the elasticity of substitution between capital and labor. This gives the desired *stock* of capital as a function of sales and the user cost of capital. Investment decisions should be aimed at achieving this optimal level of capital.

If $\sigma = 1$ (the production function is Cobb-Douglas), then

$$K_t^* = A\left(\frac{Y_t}{J_t}\right) \tag{5.7}$$

The corresponding empirical model can be specified as follows:

$$\left(\frac{I}{K}\right)_t = \beta_0 + \beta_1 \left(\frac{J}{K}\right)_t \tag{5.8}$$

where I is investment, K the beginning of period capital stock, and J a measure of the user cost of capital (see Jorgenson, 1971).

A more successful empirical specification is based on the acceleration principle, which links the demand for capital to the level or change in a firm's output. If there is no substitution between capital and labor ($\sigma = 0$), or if J_t is constant, then

$$K_t^* = A Y_t \tag{5.9}$$

Investment is then given by

$$I_t = A Y_t - (1-\delta) K_{t-1} \tag{5.10}$$

and dividing by K_{t-1} one obtains the simplest accelerator investment model:

$$\left(\frac{I_t}{K_{t-1}}\right) = \beta_0 + \beta_1 \left(\frac{Y_t}{K_{t-1}}\right) \tag{5.11}$$

This equilibrium relationship can be modified to reflect the fact that the capital stock may not adjust immediately to changes in output:

$$\left(\frac{I_t}{K_{t-1}}\right) = \beta_0 + \beta_1\left(\frac{I_{t-1}}{K_{t-2}}\right) + \beta_2\left(\frac{Y_t}{K_{t-1}}\right) + \beta_3\left(\frac{Y_{t-1}}{K_{t-2}}\right) \tag{5.12}$$

(see *e.g.* Fazzari et al., 1988).

A drawback of these models is that they are backward looking, as they do not take into account the firm's subjective expectation of the future profitability of investment projects. In addition, adjustment is instantaneous, and dynamics must be added in an *ad hoc* way.

Dynamic adjustment cost models explicitly incorporate costs of adjusting the capital stock, and thus characterize the adjustment path for capital when it is away from the static optimum level. This also results in a more explicit treatment of forward-looking expectations. The main idea is that at the optimum the increase in the value of the firm from having one additional unit of capital is equal to the cost of acquiring it.

Formally, firms maximise their net present value

$$V_t = E_t\sum_{j=0}^{\infty}\beta_{t+j}\left\{p_{t+j}\left[F\left(K_{t+j},L_{t+j}\right) - AC\left(I_{t+j},K_{t+j}\right)\right] - w_{t+j}L_{t+j} - p^I_{t+j}I_{t+j}\right\} \tag{5.13}$$

subject to

$$K_{t+j} = (1-\delta)\,K_{t+j-1} + I_{t+j} \tag{5.14}$$

where AC are the adjustment costs of investing. The Bellman equation can be written as[4]:

$$V_t\left(K_{t-1}\right) = \max_{L_t,I_t}\left\{\Pi\left(K_t,L_t,I_t\right) + \beta E_t\left[V_{t+1}\left(K_t\right)\right]\right\} \tag{5.15}$$

F.O.C.s:

$$-\left(\frac{\partial\Pi}{\partial I}\right)_t = \left(\frac{\partial\Pi}{\partial K}\right)_t + \beta E_t\left[V'_{t+1}\right] = 0 \tag{5.16}$$

[4]Note the assumption that investment occurs ath the start of the period and is immediately productive.

$$V_t' = (1-\delta)\left(\frac{\partial \Pi}{\partial K}\right)_t + (1-\delta)\beta E_t\left[V_{t+1}'\right] \tag{5.17}$$

where $V_t' = \frac{\partial V_t}{\partial K_{t-1}}$. Intuitively, (5.16) states that the marginal cost of investment (direct cost plus adjustment cost) must be equal to the marginal benefit (current increase in profits plus future increase in the value of the firm). The Euler equation (5.17) states that, along the optimal path of investment, the marginal increase in the net present value of the firm from an additional unit of capital K_{t-1} is equal to the increase in current profits plus the expect marginal increase in the future value of the firm.

Combining the two equations one obtains

$$V_t' = -(1-\delta)\frac{\partial \Pi}{\partial I_t} \tag{5.18}$$

Intuitively, the marginal increase in the value of the firm from having one additional unit of capital at $t-1$ is equal to the cost of acquiring $(1-\delta)$ units of capital at t. In other words, firms should invest up to the point where the marginal cost of investing is equal to its expected marginal benefit.

These equations do not yet provide an empirical investment model, since the shadow value V_t' is not observable. The Q model and the Euler equation model provide two approaches to make these conditions estimable.

The Q model imposes auxiliary assumptions that allow the unobservable shadow value of capital to be related to the observable ratio between the stock market's valuation of the firm and its capital stock at replacement cost. If we assume that the firm faces perfect competition in all markets, we obtain:

$$\left(\frac{\partial \Pi}{\partial I}\right)_t = -p_t\left(\frac{\partial AC}{\partial I}\right)_t - p_t^I \tag{5.19}$$

$$\left(\frac{\partial \Pi}{\partial K}\right)_t = p_t\left[\left(\frac{\partial F}{\partial K}\right)_t + \left(\frac{\partial G}{\partial K}\right)_t\right] \tag{5.20}$$

Using (5.19) in (5.18) we obtain

$$V_t' = (1-\delta)\left[p_t\left(\frac{\partial AC}{\partial I}\right)_t + p_t^I\right] \tag{5.21}$$

and therefore

$$\left(\frac{\partial AC}{\partial I}\right)_t = \left[\frac{V_t'}{(1-\delta)\, p_t^I} - 1\right]\frac{p_t^I}{p_t} = [q_t - 1]\,\frac{p_t^I}{p_t} \tag{5.22}$$

where q_t measures the ratio of the shadow value of one extra unit of capital in period t to its price. Intuitively, firms should invest up to the point where the marginal adjustment cost is exactly compensated by the net marginal benefit of investing. Note that the term in square brackets is positive if the marginal unit of capital is worth more than it costs: this net marginal benefit must exactly offset the marginal adjustment cost.

To obtain an empirical investment model, we need to specify a functional form for the adjustment cost function. Assuming a convex adjustment cost function, firms will want to smooth out investment spending as much as possible, thus being forward looking in their investment decisions. If we assume a quadratic function such as

$$AC\left(I_t, K_t\right) = \frac{b}{2}\left[\left(\frac{I}{K}\right)_t - c\right]^2 K_t \tag{5.23}$$

thus implying

$$\left(\frac{\partial AC}{\partial I}\right)_t = b\left[\left(\frac{I}{K}\right)_t - c\right] \tag{5.24}$$

$$\left(\frac{\partial AC}{\partial K}\right)_t = -b\left[\left(\frac{I}{K}\right)_t^2 - \frac{c}{2}\right] \tag{5.25}$$

we obtain that (5.22) becomes

$$b\left[\left(\frac{I}{K}\right)_t - c\right] = [q_t - 1]\,\frac{p_t^I}{p_t} \tag{5.26}$$

and

$$\left(\frac{I}{K}\right)_t = c + \frac{1}{b}\,[q_t - 1]\,\frac{p_t^I}{p_t} \tag{5.27}$$

Intuitively, given that the adjustment cost function is convex, and marginal adjustment costs are thus increasing in I, firms will want higher investment the higher the marginal increase in the net present value of the firm from an additional unit of capital relative to its replacement cost (q_t). Note that q_t reflects expectations about future profitability.

Under the assumptions that the profit function is homogeneous of degree one (sufficient conditions are competitive markets, constant return to scale, and adjustment cost function homogeneous of degree one), and the stock market is efficient, so that V_t can be measured by the stock market valuation of the company, Hayashi (1982) showed that marginal q is simply related to observable average q $\left(V_t' = \alpha\frac{V_t}{p_t^I K_{t-1}}\right)$, so that

$$\left(\frac{I}{K}\right)_t = c + \frac{1}{b}\left[\frac{V_t}{(1-\delta)\, p_t^I K_{t-1}} - 1\right]\frac{p_t^I}{p_t} = c + \frac{1}{b}Q_t \tag{5.28}$$

Note that if V_t includes debt and takes into account corporate income tax, then the tax-adjusted is (Hayashi, 1982)

$$Q_t = \left[\frac{V_t + B_t - A_t}{(1-\delta)\, p_t^I (1-\eta_t)\, K_{t-1}} - 1\right]\frac{p_t^I (1-\eta_t)}{p_t (1-\tau_t)} \tag{5.29}$$

where B_t is the market value of the firm's debt and other net liabilities, τ_t is the corporate tax rate, η_t is the present value of current and future depreciation allowances associated with an additional unit of investment in period t, and A_t is the present value of all current and future depreciation allowances that the firm can claim in respect of past investments. The intuition is that the numerator measures the market valuation of the firm's fixed capital, and the denominator measures its replacement cost value in the presence of tax.

The main difficulty with the Q model is that to obtain an observable measure of the shadow value of capital one requires strong auxiliary assumptions. In the Euler equation approach (Abel, 1980) the idea is focus on the optimal relationship between marginal adjustment costs in adjacent periods, thus not requiring measures of the shadow value.

Use (5.18) to eliminate the shadow values in (5.17), thus obtaining:

$$-\left(\frac{\partial \Pi}{\partial I}\right)_t = \left(\frac{\partial \Pi}{\partial K}\right)_t - \beta(1-\delta)\, E_t\left(\frac{\partial \Pi}{\partial I}\right)_{t+1} \tag{5.30}$$

Intuitively, along the optimal path the (net) marginal cost of investing today (net of the increase in profits through higher capital today) must be equal to the expect discounted marginal cost tomorrow.

Evaluating the expectation at realized values, under rational expectations, we obtain:

$$\beta(1-\delta)\left(\frac{\partial\Pi}{\partial I}\right)_{t+1} = \left(\frac{\partial\Pi}{\partial K}\right)_t + \left(\frac{\partial\Pi}{\partial I}\right)_t - (1-\delta)\,\varepsilon_{t+1} \tag{5.31}$$

To derive an empirical model we need to specify marginal effects in terms of observables. Assuming the profit function (5.13) and the adjustment cost function (5.23), we obtain (see Bond and Meghir, 1994):

$$\left(\frac{\partial\Pi}{\partial I}\right)_t = -b\alpha p_t\left(\frac{I}{K}\right)_t + bc\alpha p_t - p_t^I \tag{5.32}$$

$$\left(\frac{\partial\Pi}{\partial K}\right)_t = \alpha p_t\left(\frac{Y}{K}\right)_t - \alpha p_t\left(F_L\frac{L}{K}\right)_t + b\alpha p_t\left(\frac{I}{K}\right)_t^2 - bc\alpha p_t\left(\frac{I}{K}\right)_t \tag{5.33}$$

Intuitively, the marginal cost of investing is higher the higher investment (given convex adjustment costs), the higher the threshold c, and the higher the price of capital. The marginal increase in profits from an additional unit of capital is higher the higher its productivity, and the higher the adjustment costs.

Bond and Meghir (1994) show that, under these assumptions, the empirical equation under the null of no financial regimes is given by

$$\begin{aligned}\left(\frac{I}{K}\right)_{i,t} &= \beta_1\left(\frac{I}{K}\right)_{i,t-1} + \beta_2\left(\frac{I}{K}\right)_{i,t-1}^2 + \beta_3\left(\frac{CF}{K}\right)_{i,t-1} \\ &\quad + \beta_4\left(\frac{Y}{K}\right)_{i,t-1} + \beta_5\left(\frac{B}{K}\right)_{i,t-1}^2 + \alpha_i + \delta_t + u_{i,t}\end{aligned} \tag{5.34}$$

5.4 Financial Positions and Investment Decisions

The relevance of financial factors for corporate investment decisions is commonly investigated by adding financial indicators (typically cash flow) to empirical specifications derived from a real investment model. The estimated coefficients for financial indicators are interpreted as a measure of the sensitivity of investment to financial constraints. Most of the existing evidence can be traced back to the original work of Fazzari *et al.* (1988), who identified credit constrained firms on the basis of dividend pay-out behaviour, and showed that cash flows are more important for the firms a-priori considered likely to be credit constrained. Subsequent studies have generally confirmed such findings, extending the analysis along different dimensions.[5]

A common feature of the tests in this literature is that they restrict the attention to the sensitivity of investment to financial factors. The possibility that financial positions are in turn affected by investment decisions is either disregarded, or dealt with by means of instrumental variable estimation procedures. The simultaneous nature of the relationship between financial positions and investment is typically not made explicit. As pointed out by Whited (1992), existing empirical investment models are not informative about the time series interaction between a firm's balance sheet position and its investment expenditures, since they do not allow collateral to be a choice variable. In addition, existing tests are generally performed in a static, or partially dynamic, setting. This approach, however, appears unsatisfactory, given that the central idea of financial business cycle theories is the existence of a two-way dynamic interaction between firms' balance sheet positions and their investment expenditure.

On theoretical grounds it is quite natural to expect such intertemporal interactions at firm level. Investment spending is one of the determinants of firms' net worth in a medium-long term perspective, as it increases productive capacity and expected cash flows. But a causal link from investment to financial positions can also be expected to arise at business cycle frequencies. First, the presence of adjustment costs implies that a firm in need of liquid funds cannot convert capital goods into cash without suffering a loss. This type of irreversibility implies that a highly indebted firm may cut investment

[5] A number of articles have considered different data sets for the United States (Calomiris and Hubbard, 1995), countries other than the U.S. (Chirinko and Schaller, 1995; Devereux and Schiantarelli, 1990; Hoshi *et al.*, 1991; Blundell *et al.*, 1992), alternative sample split criteria to identify credit constrained firms (Whited, 1992; Oliner and Rudebush, 1992), and alternative model specifications (Bond and Meghir, 1994; Hubbard *et al.*, 1995).

in order to build up its asset base, thus making financial positions negatively related to investment decisions (see Whited, 1992). Second, and more important, a positive investment-net worth relation is a key element of the models in Kiyotaki and Moore (1997) and Kiyotaki (1997): a simultaneous relation arises since borrowers' credit limits, and thus investment, are affected by the prices of collateralized assets, while at the same time these prices are affected by the size of the credit limits.

In addition, lagged values of financial indicators may also have explanatory power for investment in a time-to-build context, while lagged values of the dependent variable allow for slow adjustment of the actual capital stock to the desired capital stock. Some evidence, although suggestive, points in this direction. Eckstein and Sinai (1986) find a systematic cyclical behaviour for alternative aggregate indicators of firms' balance sheet positions, which they interpret as supportive of a *flow of funds* cycle (see also Ciccolo, 1982; Friedman, 1982; Seth, 1992). Similar findings emerge from studies of firm-level data (e.g. Bernanke and Campbell, 1988; Bernanke *et al.*, 1990; Warshawsky, 1992).[6]

Both theoretical and empirical considerations thus suggest that the relationship between a firm's financial position and its investment expenditure is simultaneous and dynamic: over time financial conditions are affected by, and in turn affect, investment fluctuations. The natural way to test financial business cycle theories is thus by investigating the time series interaction between a firm's financial position and its investment expenditure. That is, the focus should shift from the static uni-directional causal link going from financial factors to investment, to a dynamic framework which explicitly allows for simultaneous reciprocal interactions.

The empirical analysis presented in the following sections thus estimates and tests vector autoregressions for investment and balance sheet indicators on a panel of US manufacturing firms, applying the technique proposed by Holtz-Eakin *et al.* (1985, 1988).[7] By doing so, we cast our analysis in an

[6]The analysis presented in chapter 3 found that the pattern of cyclical co-movements of the cross-section distribution of firms' financial positions is consistent with models where aggregate fluctuations are endogenously and jointly determined with financial conditions.

[7]As noted by Holtz-Eakin *et al.* (1988), although the structural interpretation of the

explicitly dynamic framework, while assuming that explanatory variables are just pre-determined rather than strictly exogenous.

5.5 Methodology and Data

This section describes the econometric methodology and the construction of the data set used in the empirical analysis. As discussed in the previous section, our objective is to characterize the dynamic interactions between investment and financial factors at firm level. A natural way to represent the dynamic relation among a set of endogenous variables is a vector autoregressive (VAR) representation:

$$Y_t = \Phi_1 Y_{t-1} + ... + \Phi_p Y_{t-p} + U \tag{5.35}$$

where Y is a vector of time series including investment, indicators of financial positions, and possibly other relevant endogenous variables, while U is a vector of disturbances. The dynamics of each endogenous variable can be characterized by the parameters of the following representation:

$$y_t = \sum_{l=1}^{p} \beta_l y_{t-l} + \sum_{l=1}^{p} \gamma_l x_{t-l} + u_t \tag{5.36}$$

where x contains lags of all remaining variables. The obvious problem in estimating such a representation at firm level is that time series on micro units are very short (our sample of U.S. manufacturing firms goes from 1981 to 1996). One of the advantages offered by panel data is that it is still possible to estimate the VAR representation by exploiting the sectional dimension. That is, equation (5.36) can be estimated by pooling time series from different units, thus assuming the following specification:

$$y_{i,t} = \sum_{l=1}^{p} \beta_l y_{i,t-l} + \sum_{l=1}^{p} \gamma_l x_{i,t-l} + u_{i,t} \tag{5.37}$$

This, however, implicitly imposes the constraint that the dynamic structure is the same for each cross sectional unit. Since individual heterogeneity is an

estimated relationship is controversial, most researchers would agree that VARs are a parsimonious and useful means of summarizing time series facts.

important feature of disaggregate data, this is a very restrictive assumption. We thus relax the pooling constraint by allowing for individual heterogeneity in both the levels and the variability of the variables examined. That is, we allow for individual effects (individual-specific intercepts) and sectional heteroskedasticity (the variance of the innovation possibly varying with the cross-section unit). Fixed firm effects are intended to account for unobserved time-invariant firm characteristics, possibly correlated with the explanatory variables, such as product demand, capital intensity, adjustment costs, and growth opportunities. In addition, we also assume the presence of fixed time-effects, intended to capture aggregate business cycle influences. We thus specify, for each of the variables of interest, the following autoregression:

$$y_{i,t} = \sum_{l=1}^{p} \beta_l y_{i,t-l} + \sum_{l=1}^{p} \gamma_l x_{i,t-l} + \mu_t + \mu_i + \eta_{i,t} \tag{5.38}$$

The presence of the lagged dependent variable, which is correlated with the firm-specific component of the error term, implies that the OLS estimator would be inconsistent even if the idiosyncratic component of the error term was serially uncorrelated. The *within* transformation, although eliminating the fixed effects, would not solve the problem, as it would introduce correlation between lagged dependent variables and the time averaged idiosyncratic error term (the same problem would occur with the random effect-GLS estimator). An alternative solution for the correlation with the fixed effects is to first difference the data, thus obtaining:

$$\Delta y_{i,t} = \sum_{l=1}^{p} \beta_l \Delta y_{i,t-l} + \sum_{l=1}^{p} \gamma_l \Delta x_{i,t-l} + \Delta\mu_t + \Delta\eta_{i,t} \tag{5.39}$$

The effect of differencing, however, is not only to eliminate the individual effects, but also to produce a first-order moving average error term. This, in turn, introduces correlation between lagged dependent variables and differenced errors, thus posing the problem of the choice of the optimal instruments. Anderson and Hsiao (1981) suggested using lagged values of differenced variables. More recently Holtz-Eakin *et al.* (1988), and Arellano and Bond (1991) have developed Generalized Method of Moments (GMM) estimators that use lagged levels of variables as instruments.[8]

The advantage of the GMM estimator is that it optimally exploits all the linear moment restrictions specified by the model. In particular, more lagged instruments become available for the differenced equations as we consider later cross-sections of the panel.[9] The number of valid instruments available in each equation differs depending on the serial correlation of the idiosyncratic component of the error term. It is thus essential to verify the assumption of serially uncorrelated errors. To this purpose, we report the m_1 and m_2 statistics, which test for first and second order serial correlation in the differenced residuals. Both statistics are asymptotically distributed as standard normal under the null of no serial correlation. If the assumption of no autocorrelation for the errors in levels is correct, so that second order lags of variables are valid instruments, the null hypothesis should be rejected for m_1 (because of the negative autocorrelation induced by first-differencing) but not for m_2. We also report p-values for the Sargan test of over-identifying restrictions, asymptotically distributed as χ^2 under the null of instrument validity, where k is the number of over-identifying restrictions.[10]

For each vector autoregression we report marginal significance values for exclusion restriction (Granger-causality) tests.[11] Since the interpretation of these tests depends crucially on the correct lag-length specification, for each lag-length we also report p-values for the test of the hypothesis that the corresponding lag can be excluded from the equation. We should emphasize that, similarly to Holtz-Eakin *et al.* (1985), we do not take sides in the debate over

---

[8] Details on the GMM estimator and test statistics can be found in Arellano and Bond (1991). In Monte Carlo simulations these authors found that the GMM estimator provides significant improvements in precision compared to simpler instrumental variables estimators.

[9] In practice, very remote lags are unlikely to be informative instruments, and hence we did not use all available moment restrictions. After some investigation we decided to use instruments dated $t-2$ and $t-3$.

[10] We also report the z_1 statistic, a Wald test of joint significance of the reported coefficients (asymptotically distributed as a χ^2_k under the null of no relationship, where k is the number of coefficients tested), and the z_2 statistic, a Wald test of the joint significance of the coefficients of the time dummies. Estimation was carried out using the DPD program (Arellano and Bond, 1988) with GAUSS version 3.2.8.

[11] For the trivariate representations, the exclusion of financial factors is tested in investment and sales equations, while the exclusion of investment is tested in the equation for the given financial indicator.

whether the results of Granger-causality tests are actually informative about causality.

As our panel data set covers many heterogeneous firms and several time periods, the disturbances can be expected to display heteroskedasticity. We thus report estimates and test results for the two-step GMM estimator, which uses the one-step residuals to form the asymptotically optimal weighting matrix.[12]

Turning to the data set, the analysis in this paper is based on company account data from Datastream International (DI). DI reports annual time series on company accounts for stock market quoted companies. Our analysis focuses on U.S. firms whose main product is in manufacturing. The initial sample included 1541 listed manufacturing firms from 1981 to 1996. The data for firms that had changed the date of their accounting year-end were adjusted at the source on a twelve-month basis.[13]

A number of selection criteria were applied to the initial sample of 1541 manufacturing firms. First, firms with some data missing were excluded from the sample. Second, all firms with less than 7 consecutive observations on each of the main variables were deleted. Third, in order to control for the impact of major mergers and acquisitions, firms whose capital stock had changed by a factor of two or more from any one year to the next were removed. Fourth, to control for outliers, we excluded firms for which any variable of interest (investment, sales, cash flow, debt-asset ratio) was more than three standard deviations away from its mean for either its own or the whole sample. The resulting panel is unbalanced both in the sense that there are more observations on some firms than on others, and in the sense that these observations may correspond to different points in time. Three cross-sections are lost in

[12]It should be noted that the asymptotic standard errors for the two-step estimator have been found in simulations to be downward biased in small samples (Arellano and Bond, 1991). This problem, however, did not appear to be present in our results.

[13]The focus of our analysis is on the behaviour of corporate leverage and cash flow, which provide a measure of the degree of firms' solvency and liquidity, respectively. The first indicator is measured with the debt-to-asset ratio, defined as Total Loan Capital (Datastream code [321]) over Total Capital Employed [322]. The second indicator is measured with free cash flow normalized by the beginning of period capital stock. The other variables are defined as folllows. Total Sales: [104]. Investment: total new fixed assets [435]. Cash Flow: provision for depreciation of fixed assets [136] + operating profit before tax [137] - total interest charges [153] - total tax charges [172]. Capital stock: book value of net total fixed assets [339].

constructing lags, a fourth by taking first differences, and a fifth by using the beginning of period capital stock. As a result, the estimation period is 1986-1996 for 461 firms, with a minimum total of 2732 observations.

5.6 Empirical Evidence

This section presents the results of our econometric investigation of the dynamic interaction between investment spending and financial conditions. The analysis is carried out in two steps. First, we focus on the dynamic interaction between investment and cash flow, and check the robustness of the results with respect to the use of alternative indicators of financial conditions. Second, we examine some of the predictions of financial business cycle theories regarding sectional and time heterogeneity.

Table 5.1 presents estimates of vector autoregressions characterizing the dynamics of the relationship between investment and cash flow.[14] We estimate two equations, one for investment and one for cash flow, where the explanatory variables are the lags of both variables. We start by assuming a lag-length p of three years. For all estimated equations the diagnostic statistics are supportive of the validity of the instruments used. The m_2 statistic does not reject the hypothesis of no second order serial correlation, while the m_1 statistic shows significant (negative) first order serial correlation. Both results are to be expected if the errors in levels are serially uncorrelated, which is a necessary condition for $t-2$ lags to be valid instruments. In addition, in all cases the Sargan test does not reject the validity of the instruments used.

Column 1 shows estimation results for the investment equation. The lag-length tests lead to reject the hypothesis that the investment equation contains less than three lags of investment and cash flow. The results of causality tests show that the hypothesis that lags of cash flow can be excluded from the investment equation can be rejected for any lag-length. The long-run effect of cash flow on investment is positive but, looking at significant coefficients only,

[14]In a comparison of the results for the three estimation methods discussed in the previous section, the GMM coefficients for the first lag of the dependent variable lie between the corresponding OLS and Within estimates, confirming the likely upward bias of OLS and downward bias of Within in the presence of firm-specific effects. We thus restrict our attention to GMM estimates in the discussion of the results.

the first lag is positive, while the third lag is negative. Column 2 presents the results of a symmetric analysis for the cash flow equation. The results of lag-length and causality tests suggest that the cash flow equation contains not more than a single lag of cash flow itself. The coefficients on lagged investment are negative but not significant at all lag-lengths.

Columns 3-5 present the estimates of trivariate vector autoregressions, obtained by including also total sales. This is done for two reasons. First, the addition of sales provides a check of the robustness of the results for the bivariate representation to the inclusion of a variable that proxies for investment opportunities which are firm and year specific (so that they cannot be captured by fixed effects). Second, it makes our dynamic specification directly comparable with the investment models traditionally used in previous empirical tests (see section 5.2). The estimates for the investment equation, in the third column, are not substantially different from those of the bivariate specification. Lags of cash flows are significant and positive as a whole, although the third lag is still significantly negative, while lagged sales do not have additional predictive power. Investment does not Granger-cause cash flow, while lags of cash flow are also significant for sales, even though causality tests in this case should be interpreted with care given that lag-length tests are marginal.

The results presented so far have examined how the availability of internal funds and investment spending interact (similar results were obtained using stock rather than flow measures of internal liquidity, such as liquid assets over total assets). However, financial business cycle theories predict that, for certain classes of firms, investment depends on both the availability of internal finance (so that indicators of *liquidity* should matter) and the access to new debt or equity finance (so that indicators of *solvency* should be relevant). The availability and cost of external finance depend, under asymmetric information, on the perceived creditworthiness of firms, which is associated to firms' net worth. Table 5.2 presents estimates of the dynamic interactions between investment and the debt-asset ratio, an indicator of solvency. The first column shows that, in the investment equation, the coefficients for lagged debt ratios are negative and significant: balance sheet positions Granger-cause investment spending. On the contrary, and similarly to the previous findings for cash flow, lagged investment has no additional predictive content for the debt-asset ratio. The results are virtually unchanged when sales are added to the explanatory variables.

Overall, these results suggest that the dynamic interaction between investment and indicators of liquidity and solvency is consistent with the hypothesis that financial positions have an important role in explaining investment fluctuations. On the other hand, lagged investment does not appear to have additional predictive content for the dynamics of cash flow or the debt-asset ratio.

One potential problem with testing the role of financial factors using liquidity or solvency measures, is that these indicators may be capturing the role of other determinants, such as expectations about the profitability of investment projects (not captured by sales or other regressors). Cash flow, for example, may be significant in investment equations just because it reflects higher expected profitability of a given investment project, rather than the role of financial constraints. The solution generally adopted in the literature is to look at some of the implications of financial business cycle theories regarding firms' heterogeneity.[15] These implications will be explored in the next sub-section.

Empirical tests of financial business cycle theories typically rely on firms' cross-sectional heterogeneity, in the sense that the behaviour of firms is expected to differ depending on the extent to which financial constraints are binding. More specifically, the sensitivity of investment spending to changes in financial positions should be higher for firms believed to face significant agency costs than for those which do not face serious agency problems. Following the approach in the seminal work by Fazzari *et al.* (1988), previous empirical studies have split the sample into groups according to a number of criteria thought a-priori to identify financially constrained firms, such as dividend policy, age, size, industrial group, bond rating, stock listing, and own-

[15] An alternative solution is to assume that investment opportunities are captured by the Q ratio (see e.g. Blundell *et al.*, 1992; Hayashi and Inoue, 1991; Schaller, 1990). However, apart from the practical consideration that the construction of Tobin's Q ratio is substantially more data demanding, it is difficult to determine the extent an average estimate of Q actually reflects expected profitabilty.

ership structure. More recently, Gertler and Gilchrist (1994) and Bernanke *et al.* (1996) have shown that, at the onset of a recession, credit-constrained firms reduce spending and production earlier and more sharply than firms with greater access to credit markets. In their study, firm size was used as a proxy for credit market access, under the assumption that small firms are more likely to be subject to credit constraints.

Tables 5.3 and 5.4 present estimates of vector autoregressions separating our sample of firms into sub-samples according to firm size and leverage, respectively. The sample split was obtained by allowing all coefficients in the estimated vector autoregressions to take different values in the two sub-samples, by interacting these terms with an appropriate dummy variable.[16] As predicted by the theory, the coefficients on lagged cash flow are significantly higher for highly leveraged firms (table 5.4). A similar pattern applies to small firms, although the differences with respect to large firms in this case are not significant (table 5.3). Overall, there appears to be substantial evidence of cross-sectional heterogeneity, consistently with the predictions of financial business cycle theories: the sensitivity of investment spending to changes in cash flow is higher for firms expected to face significant agency costs.

Although most existing empirical studies focus on cross-sectional heterogeneity, financial business cycle theories also make an important time series prediction which can be tested on panel data: financial accelerator effects are expected to be stronger the deeper the economy is in a recession, and the weaker the balance sheet of borrowers. This is so because credit constraints are likely to be binding across a wider cross section of firms in contractions than in booms.

This prediction has found some empirical support. Gertler and Hubbard (1988) re-estimated the Fazzari *et al.* (1988) investment equations, allowing liquidity effects to be different in recession years. Their results show that there is an asymmetric effect of internal net worth on investment, in the sense that cash flow effects for high-retention firms are substantially stronger in recession

[16] Lagged values of the interactions are included in the instrument set, so that this is equivalent to estimating the model separately for the two sub-samples (although imposing common error structure).

years. More recently, Kashyap *et al.* (1994) examined the cyclical behaviour of U.S. manufacturing inventories, and found that financial constraints are binding during tight-money recessionary episodes, whereas there is little evidence of inventories being sensitive to financial factors out of these episodes. Gertler and Gilchrist (1994) showed that the response of small firms to monetary policy is stronger in bad times than in good times, while no asymmetries are found for large firms.

To shed some light on the prediction of cyclical asymmetries, we turn to the following question: is the sensitivity of investment to changes in financial positions higher in bad times than in good times? Tables 5.5 and 5.6 present estimates of vector autoregressions obtained when splitting our sample into expansion and recession years, using cash flow and debt-asset ratio as financial indicators, respectively. The predictions of the theory are confirmed for both bivariate and trivariate autoregressions. The coefficients on lagged cash flow (debt-asset ratio) are significantly higher (lower) for contraction than for expansion years.

These results appear particularly interesting. They provide, for example, an explanation for the finding in Thoma (1994) that the significance of money-income causality tests across sample periods is highly correlated with the level of real activity (i.e. the money-income causality is stronger in contractions and weaker in expansions). More generally, our finding that firms' investment decisions are more sensitive to changes in financial positions during contractions suggests a natural interpretation of the empirical literature documenting the presence of various types of asymmetries in aggregate economic fluctuations (as described in chapters 1 and 2).

5.7 Summary and Conclusions

Recent financial business cycle theories based on informational asymmetries have formalized the idea that changes in financial conditions may contribute to amplify and propagate the impact of exogenous shocks on economic activity. A key feature of these theories is the existence of a two-way dynamic relationship between financial factors and investment: over time firms financial conditions are affected by, and in turn affect, investment decisions.

This chapter has argued that the natural way to investigate the predictions of financial business cycle theories at firm level is by characterizing the time series interactions between a firm's financial position and its investment expenditure. Such characterization was obtained by estimating and testing vector autoregressions on company account panel data for U.S. manufacturing firms. Our analysis thus shifted the focus from the static uni-directional causal link from financial factors to investment, to a dynamic framework which explicitly allows for simultaneous interactions.

Our results complement and extend earlier findings supporting the hypothesis that capital market imperfections have an important role in explaining aggregate cyclical dynamics. On the one hand, we find that indicators of both liquidity and solvency contain significant predictive information for investment in our sample of U.S. manufacturing firms. On the other hand, investment spending does not appear to have additional predictive content for the dynamics of either cash flow or the debt-asset ratio. These two main results are virtually unchanged when sales are added to the endogenous variables in the VAR specification.

We also find substantial evidence of cross-sectional and time heterogeneity. First, the role played by financial factors is significantly more important for highly leveraged than for low-debt firms. Second, capital market frictions have asymmetric effects, displaying a significantly larger impact in contractions than in expansions years. This latter finding suggests a natural way to interpret the recent empirical literature documenting the presence of various types of asymmetries in aggregate economic fluctuations.

Table 5.1: The dynamic relation between Investment and Cash Flow

	Dependent variable (bivariate VAR)				Dependent variable (trivariate VAR)					
Regressors	IK		CF		IK		Y		CF	
IK-1	0.15	(.00)	-0.08	(.50)	0.17	(.00)	-0.36	(.63)	-0.19	(.39)
IK-2	0.01	(.67)	-0.07	(.28)	0.03	(.07)	0.10	(.74)	0.03	(.61)
IK-3	-0.01	(.26)	-0.12	(.15)	0.00	(.88)	0.11	(.72)	-0.12	(.12)
YK-1					0.00	(.98)	0.24	(.00)	0.04	(.05)
YK-2					0.00	(.14)	-0.03	(.46)	-0.01	(.48)
YK-3					0.00	(.25)	-0.04	(.23)	0.00	(.84)
CF-1	0.03	(.00)	0.57	(.00)	0.04	(.01)	1.34	(.00)	0.42	(.00)
CF-2	0.00	(.66)	0.06	(.15)	0.01	(.10)	0.43	(.03)	0.05	(.21)
CF-3	-0.03	(.00)	0.02	(.66)	-0.01	(.04)	-0.16	(.31)	0.00	(.97)
Test statistics										
m1	(.00)		(.00)		(.00)		(.02)		(.00)	
m2	(.61)		(.50)		(.88)		(.96)		(.50)	
Sargan test	(.45)		(.86)		(.23)		(.29)		(.51)	
z1	(.00)		(.00)		(.00)		(.00)		(.00)	
z2	(.00)		(.00)		(.01)		(.01)		(.38)	
Exclude CF (p=3)	(.00)	(.00)	(.41)	(.33)	(.00)	(.00)	(.00)	(.06)	(.26)	(.48)
Exclude CF (p=2)	(.00)	(.00)	(.90)	(.50)	(.01)	(.13)	(.00)	(.31)	(.12)	(.40)
Exclude CF (p=1)	(.00)	(.00)	(.83)	(.00)	(.03)	(.00)	(.00)	(.00)	(.34)	(.00)

Notes: the sample period is 1986-1996 for 461 firms, for a total of 2732 observations. IK, CF and YK are investment, cash flow and sales, respectively, normalized by the beginning of period capital stock. Coefficients were estimated by GMM, using levels of variables dated t-2 and t-3 as instruments. Figures in parentheses are p-values of test statistics obtained with asymptotic standard errors robust to heteroskedasticity. The m1 statistic is a test for first order serial correlation in the residuals, asymptotically distributed as standard normal under the null of no serial correlation. The m2 statistic is a similar test for second order serial correlation in the residuals. The Sargan test is a test of the over-identifying restrictions, asymptotically distributed as chi2(k) under the null of instrument validity, where k is the number of over-identifying restrictions. The z1 statistic is a Wald test of joint significance of the reported coefficients, asymptotically distributed as a chi2(k) under the null of no relationship, where k is the number of coefficients tested. The z2 statistic is a Wald test of the joint significance of the coefficients of the time dummies. Exclude refers to tests of exclusion restrictions (Granger causality), while p(j) refers to a test of lag length equal to j.

Table 5.2: The dynamic relation between Investment and Leverage

	Dependent variable (bivariate VAR)				Dependent variable (trivariate VAR)					
Regressors	IK		DA		IK		Y		DA	
IK-1	0.15	(.00)	0.01	(.15)	0.13	(.00)	-1.31	(.05)	0.02	(.19)
IK-2	0.00	(.92)	0.00	(.56)	0.03	(.14)	0.23	(.39)	0.00	(.65)
IK-3	-0.02	(.17)	0.00	(.35)	0.01	(.36)	0.44	(.14)	0.00	(.41)
YK-1					0.00	(.23)	0.44	(.00)	0.00	(.89)
YK-2					0.00	(.44)	0.00	(.97)	0.00	(.75)
YK-3					0.00	(.06)	-0.06	(.02)	0.00	(.73)
DA-1	-0.15	(.02)	0.51	(.00)	-0.15	(.01)	-0.81	(.25)	0.48	(.00)
DA-2	-0.06	(.10)	0.03	(.17)	-0.06	(.07)	0.36	(.60)	0.02	(.16)
DA-3	0.13	(.03)	-0.03	(.10)	0.12	(.03)	0.93	(.02)	-0.03	(.05)
Test statistics										
m1	(.00)		(.00)		(.00)		(.01)		(.00)	
m2	(.97)		(.11)		(.61)		(.85)		(.10)	
Sargan test	(.21)		(.27)		(.29)		(.45)		(.47)	
z1	(.00)		(.00)		(.00)		(.00)		(.00)	
z2	(.01)		(.72)		(.02)		(.00)		(.54)	
Exclude DA (p=3)	(.03)	(.03)	(.15)	(.15)	(.02)	(.03)	(.02)	(.01)	(.30)	(.21)
Exclude DA (p=2)	(.04)	(.06)	(.14)	(.48)	(.03)	(.01)	(.04)	(.03)	(.24)	(.23)
Exclude DA (p=1)	(.04)	(.00)	(.06)	(.00)	(.02)	(.02)	(.02)	(.02)	(.28)	(.16)

Notes: the sample period is 1986-1996 for 461 firms, for a total of 2732 observations. IK and YK are investment and sales, normalized by the beginning of period capital stock. DA is the debt-to-asset ratio. Coefficients were estimated by GMM, using levels of variables dated t-2 and t-3 as instruments. Figures in parentheses are p-values of test statistics obtained with asymptotic standard errors robust to heteroskedasticity. Exclude refers to tests of exclusion restrictions (Granger causality), while p(j) refers to a test of lag length equal to j. For details on test statistics see notes to table 5.1.

Table 5.3: Investment-Cash Flow relation: Small vs Large firms

	Dependent variable (bivariate VAR)								Dep. variable (trivariate VAR)			
	IK				CF				IK			
Regressors	Large		Small		Large		Small		Large		Small	
IK-1	0.40	(.11)	-0.29	(.62)	-0.60	(.48)	0.95	(.67)	0.60	(.00)	-1.11	(.00)
IK-2	0.21	(.29)	-0.31	(.37)	0.08	(.89)	-0.60	(.63)	0.22	(.10)	-0.63	(.04)
IK-3	-0.19	(.28)	0.37	(.22)	-0.44	(.61)	0.90	(.52)	-0.18	(.18)	0.24	(.37)
YK-1									-0.03	(.26)	0.03	(.23)
YK-2									-0.01	(.50)	0.02	(.31)
YK-3									0.00	(.89)	-0.01	(.76)
CF-1	-0.08	(.32)	0.10	(.38)	0.78	(.02)	-0.42	(.38)	0.14	(.19)	0.11	(.33)
CF-2	-0.16	(.05)	0.19	(.06)	0.63	(.12)	-0.95	(.09)	0.08	(.37)	0.13	(.27)
CF-3	0.00	(.95)	-0.03	(.76)	-0.24	(.50)	0.43	(.35)	0.01	(.94)	-0.02	(.86)
Test statistics												
m1	-2.98	(.00)			-3.59	(.00)			-2.67	(.01)		
m2	-0.48	(.63)			0.02	(.98)			-1.52	(.13)		
Sargan test	8.78	(.79)			5.47	(.95)			16.61	(.68)		
z1	39.54	(.12)			77.22	(.00)			106.7	(.00)		
z2	20.29	(.04)			16.02	(.14)			27.85	(.00)		
z3	5.45	(.61)			7.70	(.36)			31.81	(.00)		
z4	4.85	(.30)			2.68	(.61)			3.89	(.42)		

Notes: the sample period is 1986-1996 for 461 firms, for a total of 2732 observations. IK, CF and YK are investment, cash flow and sales, respectively, normalized by the beginning of period capital stock. The sample split was obtained by interacting all regressors with a dummy variable for small firms (see section 5.5 in the text for details). Coefficients were estimated by GMM, using levels of variables dated t-2 and t-3 as instruments. Figures in parentheses are p-values of test statistics obtained with asymptotic standard errors robust to heteroskedasticity. The z3 and z4 statistics are Wald tests for small firms of joint significance of all coefficients and financial factors coefficients, respectively. For details on test statistics see notes to table 5.1.

Table 5.4: Investment-Cash Flow relation: High- vs Low-debt firms

	Bivariate autoregression								Dep. variable (trivariate VAR)			
	IK				CF				IK			
Regressors	Low debt		High debt		Low debt		High debt		Low debt		High debt	
IK-1	-0.47	(.04)	0.64	(.33)	0.54	(.65)	-1.91	(.49)	0.12	(.40)	0.19	(.57)
IK-2	-0.35	(.04)	0.38	(.53)	0.23	(.78)	-0.84	(.74)	0.00	(.98)	0.13	(.61)
IK-3	-0.17	(.23)	0.12	(.83)	0.52	(.50)	-2.64	(.41)	0.03	(.78)	-0.07	(.84)
YK-1									0.00	(.88)	0.01	(.55)
YK-2									0.00	(.55)	0.00	(.89)
YK-3									0.00	(.84)	-0.01	(.67)
CF-1	0.01	(.56)	0.08	(.71)	0.55	(.00)	0.30	(.81)	-0.01	(.78)	0.40	(.01)
CF-2	-0.03	(.17)	0.26	(.10)	-0.07	(.68)	0.47	(.66)	0.02	(.52)	0.06	(.72)
CF-3	0.00	(1.00)	0.02	(.89)	0.02	(.89)	0.27	(.75)	-0.01	(.44)	0.02	(.90)
Test statistics												
m1	1.16	(.25)			-2.52	(.01)			-2.92	(.00)		
m2	2.39	(.02)			0.07	(.95)			0.06	(.95)		
Sargan test	6.35	(.93)			5.94	(.95)			21.39	(.37)		
z1	44.10	(.00)			75.68	(.00)			110.1	(.00)		
z2	27.61	(.00)			10.88	(.45)			14.03	(.23)		
z3	14.71	(.40)			2.84	(.90)			16.93	(.08)		
z4	10.13	(.04)			1.70	(.79)			6.60	(.16)		

Notes: the sample period is 1986-1996 for 461 firms, for a total of 2732 observations. IK, CF and YK are investment, cash flow and sales, respectively, normalized by the beginning of period capital stock. The sample split was obtained by interacting all regressors with a dummy variable for high-debt firms (see section 5.5 for details). Coefficients were estimated by GMM, using levels of variables dated t-2 and t-3 as instruments. Figures in parentheses are p-values of test statistics obtained with asymptotic standard errors robust to heteroskedasticity. The z3 and z4 statistics are Wald tests for high-debt firms of joint significance of all coefficients and financial factors coefficients, respectively. For details on test statistics see notes to table 5.1.

Table 5.5: Investment-Cash Flow relation: Contractions vs Expansions

	Bivariate autoregression								Dep. variable (trivariate VAR)			
	I				CF				IK			
Regressors	Expansion		Contraction		Expansion		Contraction		Expansion		Contraction	
IK-1	-0.20	(.14)	0.52	(.24)	0.13	(.85)	-1.05	(.60)	0.00	(.99)	0.75	(.21)
IK-2	-0.11	(.28)	-0.21	(.56)	0.22	(.68)	-0.57	(.68)	-0.10	(.29)	0.32	(.53)
IK-3	0.14	(.22)	-1.03	(.08)	-0.04	(.96)	-0.77	(.80)	0.07	(.53)	-0.72	(.37)
YK-1									0.00	(.81)	-0.04	(.36)
YK-2									0.01	(.14)	-0.05	(.11)
YK-3									0.00	(.86)	0.00	(.91)
CF-1	0.02	(.54)	0.33	(.01)	0.17	(.37)	1.30	(.04)	0.00	(.98)	0.29	(.02)
CF-2	0.02	(.48)	0.00	(.96)	-0.44	(.03)	1.70	(.01)	-0.05	(.09)	0.20	(.08)
CF-3	-0.03	(.33)	0.06	(.55)	-0.12	(.52)	0.68	(.28)	-0.06	(.10)	0.15	(.17)
Test statistics												
m1	-3.45	(.00)			-2.32	(.02)			-2.90	(.00)		
m2	-0.60	(.55)			0.12	(.91)			-0.66	(.51)		
Sargan test	11.30	(.59)			7.36	(.88)			29.64	(.08)		
z1	67.36	(.00)			96.57	(.00)			69.23	(.00)		
z2	-	-			-	-			-	-		
z3	17.26	(.02)			15.63	(.03)			22.62	(.01)		
z4	13.40	(.01)			14.28	(.06)			8.36	(.08)		

Notes: the sample period is 1986-1996 for 461 firms, for a total of 2732 observations. IK, CF and YK are investment, cash flow and sales, respectively, normalized by the beginning of period capital stock. The sample split was obtained by interacting all regressors with a dummy variable for contraction years (see section 5.5 for details). Coefficients were estimated by GMM, using levels of variables dated t-2 and t-3 as instruments. Figures in parentheses are p-values of test statistics obtained with asymptotic standard errors robust to heteroskedasticity. The z3 and z4 statistics are Wald tests (for contractions years) of joint significance of all coefficients and financial factors coefficients, respectively For details on test statistics see notes to table 5.1

Table 5.6: Investment-Leverage relation: Contractions vs Expansions

	Bivariate autoregression								Dep. variable (trivariate VAR)			
	IK				DA				IK			
Regressors	Expansion		Contraction		Expansion		Contraction		Expansion		Contraction	
IK-1	0.13	(.24)	0.14	(.75)	-0.05	(.34)	0.12	(.54)	-0.31	(.40)	0.89	(.12)
IK-2	-0.12	(.35)	0.22	(.58)	-0.03	(.58)	-0.02	(.91)	-0.23	(.63)	0.51	(.29)
IK-3	0.06	(.50)	-0.26	(.51)	0.02	(.77)	-0.07	(.78)	0.00	(.96)	-0.13	(.86)
YK-1									0.03	(.00)	-0.01	(.03)
YK-2									0.02	(.05)	-0.04	(.16)
YK-3									0.00	(.73)	-0.01	(.02)
DA-1	1.09	(.01)	-2.75	(.18)	0.22	(.21)	0.23	(.73)	1.40	(.00)	-4.96	(.78)
DA-2	0.84	(.01)	-1.52	(.05)	0.20	(.21)	-0.91	(.08)	1.06	(.01)	-1.64	(.13)
DA-3	1.08	(.07)	-3.46	(.10)	-0.13	(.54)	0.42	(.50)	1.70	(.01)	-5.20	(.82)
Test statistics												
m1	-3.77	(.00)			-2.44	(.15)			-3.28	(.01)		
m2	-1.12	(2.25)			0.82	(.41)			-2.04	(.04)		
Sargan test	11.63	(.56)			7.42	(.88)			16.32	(.70)		
z1	52.61	(.00)			33.53	(.01)			46.16	(.00)		
z2	-	-			-	-			-	-		
z3	11.70	(.11)			17.48	(.02)			11.71	(.31)		
z4	6.07	(.19)			5.26	(.26)			7.78	(.10)		

Notes: the sample period is 1986-1996 for 461 firms, for a total of 2732 observations. IK and YK are investment and sales, normalized by the beginning of period capital stock. DA is the debt-to-asset ratio. The sample split was obtained by interacting all regressors with a dummy variable for contraction years (see section 5.5 for details). Coefficients were estimated by GMM, using levels of variables dated t-2 and t-3 as instruments. Figures in parentheses are p-values of test statistics obtained with asymptotic standard errors robust to heteroskedasticity. The z3 and z4 statistics are Wald tests (for contractions years) of joint significance of all coefficients and financial factors coefficients, respectively For details on test statistics see notes to table 5.1.

Chapter 6

Conclusion

Business cycles are commonly analysed within the Frisch-Slutsky analytical approach, whereby random shocks (the *impulses*) affect output through distributed-lag relationships (the *propagation mechanism*). In this framework, it is also commonly assumed that the propagation mechanism is linear and that the disturbances follow a gaussian distribution, thus imposing a symmetric behaviour over the business cycle. While much work has recently attempted to test for the presence of cyclical asymmetries and to characterize their nature, relatively less work has tried to assess the empirical significance of alternative theoretical interpretations.

This book has investigated the link between asymmetries in macroeconomic fluctuations and microeconomic changes in firms' financial conditions (the financial accelerator). The basic intuition is that financial accelerator effects can be expected to be stronger the deeper the economy is in a recession, since credit constraints are binding across a wider cross section of firms in contractions than in expansions. The book had two main objectives. On the one hand, we tried to assess at the macro level the validity of the assumption, implicit in most recent empirical analyses of aggregate fluctuations, that business cycle are all alike, and that cyclical phases are alike. On the other hand, we tried to evaluate at the micro level the empirical significance of firms' financial positions as a propagation mechanism.

We started in chapter 2 by investigating the main features of business cycles in historical perspective, complementing the analysis in the time domain with a classical analysis of individual cycles and cyclical phases, and providing formal tests of various aspects of the representative cycle hypothesis. We concluded that there is substantial heterogeneity in individual cycles and phases in terms of duration, amplitude, and co-movements between variables, and that such heterogeneity is generally statistically significant.

In chapter 3 we reported the results of an empirical investigation of business cycle asymmetries in aggregate fluctuations. We modelled the dynamics of recessions and expansions with threshold autoregressive and Markov-switching models, showing that allowing for two regimes is sufficient to account for the finding of neglected non-linearity. We concluded that business cycle asymmetries can provide both an intuitive economic interpretation and a parsimonious representation of non-linearities in macroeconomic time series.

We then applied models of explicit distribution dynamics to company account data, in chapter 4, to investigate the dynamics of the distribution of firms' financial positions and its interactions with aggregate activity. We found that the pattern of cyclical co-movements is consistent with models where aggregate fluctuations are endogenously and jointly determined with financial conditions. We also found that the dynamics of different parts of the leverage distribution contain significant predictive information for aggregate investment growth.

Finally, in chapter 5, we investigated the dynamic interaction between financial conditions and investment by estimating and testing vector autoregressions on company account panel data. We found that indicators of liquidity and solvency contain significant predictive information for investment at firm level. We also found evidence of both cross-sectional and time heterogeneity: the role played by financial factors is significantly more important for high-leverage than for low-debt firms, while capital market frictions displaying a larger impact in contractions than in expansions.

Overall, our analysis of macroeconomic data leads us to conclude that both the *representative cycle* and the *representative phase* hypotheses can be rejected, while our analysis of microeconomic data supports the hypothesis that agents' financial positions have an important role for aggregate cyclical dynamics.

These results have important empirical and theoretical implications. At the empirical level, our findings suggest that describing business cycles in terms of sample second moments, while imposing symmetric behaviour between expansions and contractions, is likely to lead to a substantial loss of information. At the theoretical level, the rejection of the representative cycle hypothesis underlines the difficulties of developing theories providing a unified explanation of *the* business cycle, while suggesting a research strategy focusing on the interactions between agents' distribution dynamics at the micro level and aggregate fluctuations.

Checking the robustness of our empirical results and sharpening the theoretical links between the role of financial constraints at the micro level and cyclical asymmetries at the macro level are important objectives of the current economic research agenda.

Bibliography

Chapter 1

Acemoglu, D. and Scott, A. (1997), "Asymmetric Business Cycles: Theory and Time-Series Evidence", *Journal of Monetary Economics*, 40(3), 501-33.

Ball, L. and Mankiw, N.G. (1994), "Asymmetric Price Adjustment and Economic Fluctuations", *Economic Journal*, 104(423), 247-61.

Bernanke, B. and Gertler, M. (1989) "Agency Costs, Net Worth, and Business Fluctuations", *American Economic Review*, 79(1), March 1989, pages 14-31.

Blanchard, O.J., and Fischer S. (1989), *Lectures on macroeconomics*, MIT Press, Cambridge, Massachussets.

Burns, A.F. and Mitchell W.C. (1946), *Measuring business cycles*, New York: NBER.

Caballero, R. J. and Engel, E. M. (1993), "Microeconomic Rigidities and Aggregate Price Dynamics", *European Economic Review*, 37(4), 697-711.

Fazzari, S., Hubbard, R. and Petersen, B. (1988), "Financing Constraints and Corporate Investment", *Brookings Papers on Economic Activity*, 0(1), 41-95.

Gallegati, M. and Stanca, L.M. (1998), *Le Fluttuazioni Economiche in Italia, 1861-1995*, Torino, Giappichelli.

Gertler, M. and Gilchrist, S. (1994), "Monetary Policy, Business Cycles, and the Behaviour of Small Manufacturing Firms", *Quarterly Journal of Economics*, 109(2), 309-340.

Gertler, M. and Hubbard, R. (1988), "Financial Factors in Business Fluctuations", in *Financial market volatility: A symposium*, Federal Reserve Bank of Kansas City Symposium Series, Kansas City, 33-71.

Greenwald, B. and Stiglitz, J. (1993) "Financial Market Imperfections and Business Cycles", *Quarterly Journal of Economics*, 108, 77-114.

Kashyap, A., Lamont, O. and Stein, J. (1994), "Credit Conditions and the Cyclical Behavior of Inventories", *Quarterly Journal of Economics*, 109(3), 565-92.

Kiyotaki, N., Moore, J. (1997), "Credit Cycles", *Journal of Political Economy*, 105(2), 211-48.

Koopmans, T.C. (1947), "Measurement without Theory", *Review of Economics and Statistics*, n. 29, 163-174.

Lucas, R.E. (1977), "Understanding Business Cycles." in D. Brunner e A.H. Meltzer (ed), *Stabilization of the Domestic and International Economy*, Amsterdam, North Holland.

Mittnik, S. and Niu, Z. (1994), "Asymmetries in Business Cycles: Econometric Techniques and Empirical Evidence", in Semmler W. Eds. *Business Cycles: Theory and Empirical Methods*, Kluwer Academic Publishers, Boston, 331-50.

Pfann, G.A. (1993), "The Thin End of the Wedge: Non-linearity in Stochastic Labor Market Dynamics", in van-Ours, J.C., Pfann, G.A., and Ridder, G. eds. *Labor demand and equilibrium wage formation*, North-Holland, New York, 1-26.

Potter, S. (1994) "Asymmetric economic propagation mechanism", in Semmler W. Eds. *Business Cycles: Theory and Empirical Methods*, Kluwer Academic Publishers, Boston, 313-330.

Prescott, E.C. (1986), "Theory ahead of business cycle measurement", *Federal Reserve Bank of Minneapolis Quarterly Review*, 10, 9-22.

Quah, D. (1995), "Business Cycle Empirics: Calibration and Estimation: An Introduction", *Economic Journal*, 105(433), 1594-96.

Romer, D. (1996), *Advanced macroeconomics*, New York: McGraw-Hill Companies.

Sargent, T.J. (1979), *Macroeconomic theory*, New York, London: Academic Press.

Sargent, T., Sims C. (1977), "Business Cycle Modelling without Pretending to Have Too Much A Priori Economic Theory", in Sims, C.A. (ed.) *New Methods in Business Cycle Research*, Federal Reserve Bank of Minneapolis, Minneapolis.

Stanca, L.M. (1998), "The postwar stabilization of economic fluctuations: evidence from a chain index of Italian GDP", *Rivista Internazionale di Scienze Sociali*, 106(1), 89-114.

Stanca, L.M. (1999a), "Le fluttuazioni economiche in Italia: un riesame dell'ipotesi del ciclo rappresentativo (1861-1992)", *Rivista di Politica Economica*, 89(3), 3-44.

Stanca, L.M. (1999b), "Are business cycles all alike? Evidence from long run international data", *Applied Economics Letters*, 6, 765-769.

Stanca, L. (1999c), "Asymmetries and Non-linearities in the Italian business cycle", *Applied Economics*, 31, 483-91.

Stanca, L., Delli Gatti, D. and Gallegati, M. (1999), "Financial fragility, heterogeneous agents, and aggregate fluctuations: evidence from a panel of U.S. firms", *Applied Financial Economics*, 9, 87-99.

Stanca, L. and Gallegati, M. (1999), "The dynamic relation between financial conditions and investment: evidence from panel data", *Industrial and Corporate Change*, 8(3), 551-572.

Chapter 2

Ancona, A. and Bonato, L. (1996), "Ciclo economico e stabilizzazione. La storia recente in un confronto internazionale", *Rivista di Politica Economica*, 58(3), 3-35.

Ardeni and P.G., Gallegati, M. (1991), "Long-term trends and cycles in the Italian Economy (1961-1988)", *Giornale degli economisti*, 193-235.

Ardeni, P. and Gallegati, M. (1994), "Cicli di crescita nello sviluppo: 1861-1990", in P. Ciocca (ed.), *Il progresso economico dell'Italia*, Il Mulino, Bologna.

Backus, D.K. and Kehoe, P.J. (1992), "International evidence on the historical properties of business cycles", *American Economi Review*, 82, 864-888.

Baily, M. (1978), "Stabilization Policy and Private Economic Behavior", *Brookings Papers on Economic Activity*, (1), 11-60.

Baxter, M., King, R. (1995), "Measuring Business Cycles Approximate Band-Pass Filters for Economic Time Series", National Bureau of Economic Research Working Paper 5022.

Blackburn, K. and Ravn, M.O. (1992), "Business Cycles in the United Kingdom: Facts and Fictions", *Economica*, 59 (236), 383-401.

Blanchard, O.J. and Watson, M.W. (1986), "Are business cycles all alike?", in R. Gordon (ed.) *The American business cycle: continuity and change*, Chicago, University of Chicago Press, 166-178.

Bronfenbrenner, M. (1969), *Is the Business Cycle Obsolete?*, based on a conference of the Social Science Research Council Committee on Economic Stability.

Bry G., Boschan C. (1971), "Cyclical Analysis of Times Series: Selected Procedures and Computer Programs" (New York: NBER, Technical Paper No.20.

Canova, F. (1998), "Detrending and Business Cycle Facts", *Journal of Monetary Economics*, 41(3), 475-512.

Canova, F. (1998), "Does Detrending Matter for the Determination of the Reference Cycle and the Selection of Turning Points?", *Economic Journal*, 109(452), 126-50.

Caselli, G.P. and Marinelli, L. (1994), "Italian GNP Growth 1890-1992: A Unit Root or Segmented Trend Representation?", *Economic Notes*, 23(1), 53-73.

Chiarini, B. (1994), "Trends, effetti permanenti e componenti non stazionarie: uno studio disaggregato del prodotto e dell'occupazione italiana", *Rivista di Politica Economica*, 84,39-80.

Cogley, T., Nason, J. (1995) "Effects of the Hodrick-Prescott Filter on Trend and Difference Stationary Time Series: Implications for Business Cycle Research", *Journal of Economic Dynamics and Control*, 19(1-2), 253-78.

Correia, I., Neves, J. and Rebelo, S. (1992), "Business Cycles from 1850 to 1950. New Facts about Old Data", *European Economic Review*, 37, 459-467.

Croce, G. (1996), "Fluttuazioni del prodotto e persistenza: Una verifica per l'Italia", *Economia Internazionale*, 49(2), 177-95.

Danthine, J. and Girardine, M. (1989), "Business Cycles in Switzerland: A Comparative Study", *European Economic Review*, 33(1), 31-50.

De Long B. and Summers, L. (1986), "The Changing Cyclical Variability of economic Activity in the United States" in R. Gordon (ed.) *The American business cycle: continuity and change*, Chicago, University of Chicago Press, 679-733.

Diebold, F.X, and Rudebusch, G.D. (1990) "A Nonparametric Investigation of Duration Dependence in the American Business Cycle", *Journal of Political Economy*, 98, 3.

Diebold, F.X., and Rudebusch, G.D. (1992), "Have postwar economic fluctuations been stabilized?", *American Economic Review*, 82, 993-1005.

Dolado, J.J., Sebastian, M. andValles, J. (1993), "Cyclical patterns of the Spanish economy", in *Changes in the business cycle and the implications for monetary policy*, Bank for International Settlements, 4.

Englund, P., Persson, T. and Svensson, L. (1992), "Swedish Business Cycles: 1861-1988", *Journal of Monetary Economics*, 30, 343-71.

Ercolani, P. (1978), "Documentazione statistica di base", in Fuà G. (a cura di), *Lo sviluppo economico in Italia*, vol. III, Milano, Angeli.

Fenoaltea, S. (1987), "Le costruzioni in Italia, 1861-1913", *Rivista di storia economica*, n.s., Febrary, Vol.4.

Fiorito, R. and Kollintzas T. (1994), "Stylized facts of business cycles in the G7 from a real business cycles perspective", *European Economic Review*, 38(2), 235-69.

Fratianni, M. and Spinelli, F. (1997), *A monetary history of Italy*, Cambridge, Cambridge University Press.

Fuà, G. (1978), *Lo sviluppo economico in Italia*, vol.III, Studi di settore e documentazione di base, Franco Angeli, Milano, terza edizione (prima edizione: 1969).

Fuà, G. (1981), *Lo Sviluppo Economico in Italia*, vol. I, Milano, Angeli.

Fuà, G. and Gallegati Mauro. (1996), "An annual chain index of Italy's real product, 1861-1989", *Review of Income and Wealth*, 42(2).

Gallegati, Marco. (1996), "Testing output stationarity through its supply components: Italy (1861-1893)", *Economic Notes*, 25, 249-260.

Gallegati, Marco and Gallegati, Mauro (1995), "Volatilità e persistenza delle fluttuazioni: un'analisi di lungo periodo di alcune serie individuali di produzione in Italia, 1890-1985", *Giornale degli Economisti e Annali di Economia*, 53(1-3), 81-99.

Gerschenkron, A. *Economic Backwardness in Historical Perspective*, Belknap-Harvard, Cambridge (Mass.) 1962.

Golinelli, R. and Monterastelli, M. (1990), "Un metodo per la ricostruzione di serie storiche compatibili con la nuova contabilità nazionale (1951-1989)", Nota di lavoro n. 9001, Prometeia, Bologna.

Goodwin, R. (1955), "A model of cyclical growth", in E.Lundberg (ed.), *The Business Cycle in the Post War World*, London: MacMillan, 203-221.

Guay, A., St-Amant, P. (1997), "Do the Hodrick-Prescott and Baxter-King filters provide a good approximation of Business Cycles", CREFE Working Paper No. 53.

Hassler, P., Lundvik, P., Persson, T. and Soderlind, P. (1994), "The Swedish business cycle: stylized facts over 130 years", in Bergstrom V. e Vredin A., *Measuring and Interpreting Business Cycles*, Clarendon Press, Oxford.

Hicks, J. (1950), *A Contribution to the Theory of the Trade Cycle*, Oxford, Clarendon.

Hodrick, R.J. and Prescott, E.J. (1980), "Post-war US business cycles: an empirical investigation", Discussion Paper 451, Carnegie-Mellon University.

Istituto Centrale di Statistica (1957), "Indagine statistica sullo sviluppo del reddito nazionale in Italia dal 1861 al 1956", Annali di Statistica, Serie VIII, Vol. IX.

Istituto Centrale di Statistica (1986), "Annuario di contabilità nazionale", Cap. 7: Dati retrospettivi, Roma, ISTAT.

Kaldor, N. (1954), "The relationship of economic growth and cyclical fluctuations", *Economic Journal*, 64, 53-71.

King, R. and Rebelo, S. (1993), "Low Frequency Filtering and Real Business Cycles", *Journal of Economic Dynamics and Control*, 17(1-2).

Kydland, F.E. and Prescott, E.C. (1990), "Business cycles: real facts and a monetary myth", *Federal Reserve Bank of Minneapolis Quarterly Review*, Spring, 3-18.

Liesner, T. (1989), *One hundred years of economic statistics : United Kingdom, United States of America, Australia, Canada, France, Germany, Italy, Japan, Sweden.* London, Economist Publications.

Lucas, R.E. (1977), "Understanding Business Cycles." in D. Brunner e A.H. Meltzer (ed), *Stabilization of the Domestic and International Economy*, Amsterdam, North Holland.

Maddison, A. (1991), "A Revised Estimate of Italian Economic Growth", *BNL Quarterly Review*, 177, 225-41.

Maddison, A. (1995), *Monitoring the world economy, 1820-1992*, Development Centre of the Organisation for Economic Co-operation and Development, 1995.

Mitchell, B.R. (1993), *International historical statistics.* Europe 1750-1988, 3rd ed.

Neftci, S.N. (1984), "Are economic time series asymmetric over the business cycle?", *Journal of Political Economy*, 92, 307-328.

Pistoresi, B. (1996), "Radici unitarie e persistenza: l'analisi univariata delle fluttuazioni economiche", *Rivista di Politica Economica*, 59, 111-152.

Prescott, E.C. (1986), "Theory ahead of business cycle measurement", *Federal Reserve Bank of Minneapolis Quarterly Review*, 10, 9-22.

Rey, G. (1991), *I conti economici dell'Italia - Una sintesi delle fonti ufficiali*, Laterza, 1991.

Romer, C. (1986), Is the Stabilization of the Postwar Economy a Figment of the Data? *American Economic Review*, 76, pp.314-34.

Romer, C. (1989), The Prewar Business Cycle Reconsidered: New Estimates of Gross National Product, 1869-1908, *Journal of Political Economy*, 97, 1-37.

Rossi, N., Sorgato, A. and Toniolo, G. (1993), "I conti economici italiani: una ricostruzione statistica, 1890-1990", *Rivista di Storia Economica*, 10(1).

Saint-Paul G. (1997), "Business cycles and long-run growth", *Oxford Review of Economic Policy*, 13(3), 145-153.

Sheffrin, S. (1988), Have economic fluctuations been dampened?, *Journal of Monetary Economics*, 21, 73-83.

Schlitzer, G. (1993), "Business Cycles in Italy: A Retrospective Investigation", Banca d'Italia, Temi di Discussione, N. 211.

Schlitzer, G. (1995), "Have Economic Fluctuations Been Dampened? New Empirical Evidence from Italy", *Open Economies Review*, 6, 387-397.

Schumpeter, J.A. (1939), *Business Cycles: A theoretical, historical and statistical analysis of the capitalist process*, 2 vols., New York: McGraw-Hill.

Sichel, D.E.(1993): "Business cycle asymmetry: a deeper look", *Economic Inquiry*, 31, 224-236.

Stanca, L.M. (1996), "La misurazione del ciclo economico, aspetti metodologici e regolarità empiriche per l'economia italiana (1960-93)", *Giornale degli Economisti ed Annali di Economia*, 55(2), 211-241.

Stanca, L.M. (1998), "The postwar stabilization of economic fluctuations: evidence from a chain index of Italian GDP", *Rivista Internazionale di Scienze Sociali*, 106(1), 89-114.

Stanca, L.M. (1999a), "Le fluttuazioni economiche in Italia: un riesame dell'ipotesi del ciclo rappresentativo (1861-1992)", *Rivista di Politica Economica*, 89(3), 3-44.

Stanca, L.M. (1999b), "Are business cycles all alike? Evidence from long run international data", *Applied Economics Letters*, 6, 765-769.

Stock, J., Watson, M. (1998), "Business cycle fluctuations in U.S. macroeconomic time series", NBER Working Paper No. 6528.

Taylor, J. (1986), "Improvements in Macroeconomic Stability: The Role of Wages and Prices", in R. Gordon (ed.) *The American business cycle: continuity and change*, Chicago, University of Chicago Press, p. 641-677.

Toniolo, G. (1978), (a cura di), *L'economia italiana (1861-1940)*, Bari, Laterza.

Watson, M. (1994), "Business Cycle Duration and Postwar Stabilization of the U.S. Economy", *American Economic Review*, 84(1), 24-46.

Zamagni, V. (1993), *The economic history of Italy, 1860-1990*, Oxford, Clarendon Press.

Zarnowitz, V. (1992), "Facts and Factors in the Modern Evolution of U.S. Economic Fluctuations", in *Business Cycles: Theory, History, Indicators, and Forecasting*, Univ. of Chicago Press.

Zarnowitz, V. and Moore, G. (1986), "Major Changes in Cyclcal Behaviour", in R. Gordon (ed.) *The American business cycle: continuity and change*, University of Chicago Press, p. 519-582.

Chapter 3

Acemoglu D. and Scott A. (1994), "Asymmetries in the cyclical behaviour of UK labour markets", *Economic Journal*, 102, 1303-1323.

Anderson, T.W. and Goodman, L.A. (1957), "Statistical Inference about Markov Chains", *Annals of Mathematical Statistics*, 28, 89-110.

Blatt, J.M. (1980), "On the Frisch Model of the Business Cycle", *Oxford Economic Papers*, 32, 467-479.

Beaudry, P. and Koop, G. (1993), "Do recessions permantly change output?", *Journal of Monetary Economics*, 31 149-163.

Boldin, M. (1992), "Using switching models to study business cycle asymmetries: overview of methodology and application", Federal Reserve Bank of New York, Research Paper No. 9211.

Brock, W. and Potter, S. (1993), "Nonlinear Time Series and Macroeconometrics", in *Handbook of Statistics*, Vol. II, G.S. Maddala, C.R. Rao and H.D. Vinod (Eds.), Elsevier, Amsterdam..

Brock, W.A., Dechert, W.D., Scheinkman J.A., and Lebaron, D. (1996), "A Test for Independence Based on the Correlation Dimension", *Econometric Reviews* , 15 197-235.

Brunner, A.D. (1992), "Conditional Asymmetries in Real GNP: A seminonparametric Approach", *Journal of Business and Economic Statistics*, 10, 65-72.

Delong, B. and Summers, L. (1986), "Are business cycles Symmetric?", in R. Gordon (ed.) *The American business cycle: continuity and change*, Chicago, University of Chicago Press, 166-178.

Diebold, F.X. and Rudebusch, G.D. (1990), "A Nonparametric Investigation of Duration Dependence in the American Business Cycle", *Journal of Political Economy*, 98, 3.

Engle, R.F. (1982), "Autoregressive conditional heteroscedasticity with estimates of the variance of United Kingdom inflation", *Econometrica*, 50, 987-1007.

Falk, B. (1986), "Further Evidence on the Asymmetric Behavior of Economic Time Series over the Business Cycle", *Journal of Political Economy*, 94, 1096-1109.

French, M.W., Sichel D.E. (1993), "Cyclical Patterns in the Variance of Economic Activity", *Journal of Business and Economic Statistics*, 11, 113-119.

Garcia, R. and Perron, P. (1996), "An analysis of the real interest rate under regime shifts", *Review of Economics and Statistics*, 58, 111-125.

Granger, C.W. and Terasvirta, T. (1993) *Modelling Nonlinear Economic Relationships*, Oxford University Press.

Goodwin, R. (1955), "A model of cyclical growth", in E.Lundberg (ed.), The *Business Cycle in the Post War World*, London: MacMillan, 203-221.

Hamilton, J.D. (1989), "A New Approach to the Economic Analysis of Nonstationary Time Series and the Business Cycle", *Econometrica* 57, 357-384.

Hamilton, J.D. (1990), "Analysis of Time Series subject to changes in regime", *Journal of Econometrics*, 45, 39-70.

Hansen, B.E. (1992), "The Likelihood Ratio Test Under Non-Standard Conditions: Testing the Markov Trend Model of GNP", *Journal of Applied Econometrics*, 7, 561-582.

Hicks, J. (1950), *A Contribution to the Theory of the Trade Cycle*, Oxford, Clarendon.

Holly S. and Stannett, M. (1995), "Are there asymmetries in UK consumption? A time series analysis", *Applied Economics*, 27, 767-72.

Hussey, R. (1992), "Nonparametric Evidence on Asymmetry in Business Cycles Using Aggregate Employment Time Series", *Journal of Econometrics*, 51, 217-231.

Istituto Centrale di Statistica (1986) *Annuario di contabilita nazionale*, Cap. 7: Dati retrospettivi, Roma, ISTAT.

Kaldor, N. (1954), "The relationship of economic growth and cyclical fluctuations", *Economic Journal*, 64, 53-71.

Keynes, J.M. (1936) *The General Theory of Employment, Interest and Money*, London: Macmillan.

Krager, H. (1992), "Modelling cyclycal asymmetry in a production series using threshold autoregressive models", *Recherches Economiques de Louvain*, 58, 473-486.

Lam, P.S. (1990), "The Hamilton Model with a General Autoregressive Component: Estimation and Comparison with Other Models of Economic Time Series", *Journal of Monetary Economics* 26, 409-432.

Lee, T., White, H. and Granger, C.W. (1993), "Testing for neglected non-linearity in time series models: a comparison of nural network methods and alternative test", *Journal of Econometrics*, 56, 269-290.

Luukkonen, R., Saikkonen, P. and Teraasvirta T. (1988), "Testing linearity against smooth transition autoregressive models", *Biometrika*, 75, 491-499.

McLeod, A.J., and Li, W.K. (1983), "Diagnostic checking ARMA time series models using squared-residuals correlations", *Journal of Time Series Analysis*, 4, 269-273.

McNevin, B., Neftci, S.N. (1992), "Some Evidence on the Non-Linearity of Economic TIme Series: 1890-1981", in Benhabib, J. (Ed.) *Cycles and chaos in economic equilibrium*, Princeton University Press, 1992, 429-45.

McQueen, G. and Thorley, S. (1993), "Asymmetric business cycle turning points", *Journal of Monetary Economics*, 31, 341-362.

Mills, T.C. (1995), "Business cycle asymmetries and non-linearities in U.K. macroeconomic time series", *Ricerche Economiche*, 49, 97-124.

Mitchell, W. (1927) *Business Cycles: The Problem and Its Setting*, New York: NBER.

Neftci, S.N. (1984), "Are economic time series asymmetric over the business cycle?", *Journal of political economy*, 92, 307-328.

Newey, W. and West, K. (1987), "A Simple Positive Semi-Definite Heteroskedasticity and Autocorrelation Consistent Covariance Matrix", *Econometrica*, 55, 703-08.

Peel, D. and Speight, A.E. (1996), "Is the US Business Cycle Asymmetric? Some further evidence", *Applied Economics*, 28, 405-415.

Potter, S. (1994), "Asymmetric economic propagation mechanism", in Semmler W. Eds. *Business Cycles: Theory and Empirical Methods*, Kluwer Academic Publishers, Boston, 313-330.

Potter, S. (1995), "A nonlinear approach to US GNP", *Journal of Applied Econometrics*, 10, 109-125.

Rossi, N., Sorgato, A. and Toniolo, G. (1993), "I conti economic italiani: una ricostruzione statistica, 1890-1990", *Rivista di Storia Economica*, 10, 1-47.

Rothman, P. (1991), "Further Evidence on the Asymmetric Behaviour of Unemployment Rates over the Business Cycle", *Journal of Macroeconomics*, 13, 291-298.

Schumpeter, J. (1939) *Business Cycles: A theoretical, historical and statistical analysis of the capitalist process*, 2 vols., New York: McGraw-Hill.

Schwarz, G. (1978), "Estimating the Dimension of a Model", *Annals of Mathematical Statistics*, 6, 461-464.

Sichel, D.E. (1989), "Are Business Cycles Asymmetric? A correction", *Journal of Political Economy*, 97, 1255-1260.

Sichel D.E.(1993), "Business cycle asymmetry: a deeper look", *Economic Inquiry*, 31, 224-236.

Stanca, L. (1999c), "Asymmetries and Non-linearities in the Italian business cycle", *Applied Economics*, 31, 483-91.

Stock, J.H. (1987), "Measuring Business Cycle Time", *Journal of Political Economy*, 95,1240-61.

Subba Rao, T. and Gabr, M. (1984), "An Introduction to Bispectral Analysis and Bilinear Time Series Models", Lecture Notes in Statistics, 24, Springer Verlag, New York.

Terasvirta, T. and Anderson, H. (1992), "Modelling Nonlinearities in business cycles using smooth transition autoregressive models", *Journal of Applied Econometrics*, 7, S119-S136.

Tong, H (1983), "Threshold models in non-linear time series analysis", Lecture Notes in Statistics, No.21, Springer, Heidelberg.

Tong, H. (1990) *Nonlinear time series: a dynamical system approach*, Oxford University Press.

Tsay, R.S. (1989), "Testing and modelling threshold autoregressive processes", *Journal of the American Statistical Association*, 84, 231-40.

Weiss, A. (1986), "ARCH and bilinear time series models: comparison and combination", *Journal of Business and Economic Statistics*, 4, 59-70.

Westlund, A.H, and Ohlen, S. (1991), "On Testing for Symmetry in Business Cycles", *Empirical Economics*, 16, 479-502.

Chapter 4

Bernanke, B. and Blinder, A. (1988), "Credit, Money, and Aggregate Demand", *American Economic Review*, 98, 435-439.

Bernanke, B. and Gertler, M. (1989), "Agency Costs, Net Worth, and Business Fluctuations", *American Economic Review*, 79(1), 14-31.

Bernanke, B. and Gertler, M. (1990), "Financial Fragility and Economic Performance", *Quarterly Journal of Economics*, 105, 14-31.

Bernanke, B., Gertler, M., and Gilchrist, S. (1996), "The Financial Accelerator and the Flight to Quality", *The Review of Economics and Statistics*, 78(1), 1-15.

Bernanke, B. and Campbell, J. (1988), "Is There a Corporate Debt Crisis?", *Brookings Papers on Economic Activity*, 1:1988, 83-125.

Bernanke, B. and Campbell, J. (1990), "U.S. Corporate Leverage: Developments in 1987 and 1988", *Brookings Papers on Economic Activity*, 1:1990, 255-287.

Ciccolo, J.H. (1982), "Changing Balance Sheet Relationships in the U.S. Manufacturing Sector, 1926-1977", *The changing roles of debt and equity in financing U.S. capital formation.* (Ed.), University of Chicago Press, Chicago, 65-74.

Delli Gatti, D., and Gallegati, M. (1996), "Financial Market Imperfections and Irregular Growth Cycles", *Scottish Journal of Political Economy*, 43(2), 146-58.

Delli Gatti, D., Gallegati, M. and Gardini, L. (1993), "Investment Confidence, Corporate Debt and Income fluctuations", *Journal of Economic Behaviour and Organization*,.3, 327-354.

Eckstein, O. and Sinai, A. (1986), "The Mechanisms of the Business Cycle in the Postwar Era", in *The American business cycle: Continuity and change*, (Ed.) R. Gordon, National Bureau of Economic Research Studies in Business Cycles series, vol. 25, Chicago and London: University of Chicago Press, 39-105.

Fazzari, S., Hubbard, R. and Petersen, B. (1988), "Financing Constraints and Corporate Investment", *Brookings Papers on Economic Activity*, 1, 141-95.

Franke, R. and Semmler, W. (1989), "Debt-Financing of Firms, Stability and Cycles in a Dynamica Macroeconomic Growth Model", in W. Semmler (ed.), *Financial Dynamics and business Cycles*, M.E. Sharpe, Armonk, N.Y.

Friedman B.M. (1982), "Debt and Economic Activity in the United States", in *The changing roles of debt and equity in financing U.S. capital formation,* (Ed.) B.M. Friedman, University of Chicago Press, Chicago, pp. 91-110.

Gertler, M. (1988), "Financial Structure and Aggregate Economic Activity: An Overview", *Journal of Money, Credit and Banking*, 20(3), 559-588.

Gertler, M. and Gilchrist, S. (1994), "Monetary Policy, Business Cycles, and the Behaviour of Small Manufacturing Firms", *Quarterly Journal of Economics*, 109(2), 309-340.

Gertler, M. and Hubbard, R. (1988), "Financial Factors in Business Fluctuations", in *Financial market volatility: A symposium*, Federal Reserve Bank of Kansas City Symposium Series, Kansas City, pp. 33-71.

Greenwald, B. and Stiglitz, J. (1993), "Financial Market Imperfections and Business Cycles", *Quarterly Journal of Economics*, 108, 77-114.

Kashyap, A., Lamont, O. and Stein, J. (1994), "Credit Conditions and the Cyclical Behavior of Inventories", *Quarterly Journal of Economic*, 109(3), 565-92.

Kindleberger, C.P. (1978), *Manias, Panics and Crashes. A History of Financial Crises*, Basic Books, New York.

Kiyotaki, N. and Moore, J. (1997), "Credit Cycles", *Journal of Political Economy*, 105(2), 211-48.

Minsky, H.P. (1982), *Can It Happen Again? Essays on Instability and Finance*, Armonk N.Y. M.E. Sharpe.

Myers, S. and Majluf, N. (1984), "Corporate financing and investment decisions when firms have information that investors do not have", *Journal of Financial Economics*, 13, 187-221.

Quah D. (1994), "One Business Cycle and One Trend from (Many,) Many Disaggregates", *European Economic Review*, 38(3-4), 605-13.

Quah D. (1996a), "Aggregate and regional disaggregate fluctuations", *Empirical Economics*, March 1996, 21(1), 137-159

Quah D. (1996b), "Empirics for economic growth and convergence", *European Economic Review*, 40(6), 1353-1375.

Seth, R. (1992), "Corporate Leverage and the Business Cycle", *Contemporary Policy Issues*, 10, 65-80.

Stanca, L., Delli Gatti, D. and Gallegati, M. (1999), "Financial fragility, heterogeneous agents, and aggregate fluctuations: evidence from a panel of U.S. firms", *Applied Financial Economics*, 9, 87-99.

Taylor, L. and O'Connell, S. (1985), "A Minsky Crisis", *Quarterly Journal of Economics*, 100, p. 871-885.

Warshawsky, M. (1992), "Is There a Corporate Debt Crisis? Another Look", in *Financial Markets and Financial Crises*, (Ed.) G. R. Hubbard, National Bureau of Economic Research, University of Chicago Press, Chicago, 207-230.

Chapter 5

Abel, A. (1980), "Empirical investment equations: an integrative approach", in K. Brunner and A. Meltzer (eds.), *On the State of Macroeconomics*, *Carnegie-Rochester Conference Series*, 12, 39-93.

Anderson, T. and Hsiao, C. (1981), "Formulation and estimation of dynamic models using panel data", *Journal of Econometrics*, Vol. 18, 47-82.

Arellano, M. and Bond, S. (1988), "Dynamic panel data estimation using DPD - a guide for users", Institute for Fiscal Studies Working paper, No. 88/15.

Arellano, M. and Bond, S. (1991), "Some tests of specification for panel data: Monte Carlo evidence and an application to employment equations", *Review of Economic Studies*, 58, 277-297.

Bernanke, B. and Campbell, J. (1988) "Is There a Corporate Debt Crisis?", *Brookings Papers on Economic Activity*, 1, 83-125.

Bernanke, B., Campbell, J. and Whited, T. (1990), "U.S. Corporate Leverage: Developments in 1987 and 1988", *Brookings Papers on Economic Activity*, 1, 255-287.

Bernanke, B. and Gertler, M. (1989), "Agency Costs, Net Worth, and Business Fluctuations", *American Economic Review*, 79(1), 14-31.

Bernanke, B., Gertler, M., and Gilchrist, S. (1996), "The Financial Accelerator and the Flight to Quality", *The Review of Economics and Statistics*, 78(1), 1-15.

Blundell, R., Bond, S., Devereux, M. and Schiantarelli, F. (1992), "Investment and Tobins Q", *Journal of Econometrics*, 51, 233-257.

Bond, S. and Meghir, C. (1994), "Dynamic investment models and the firms financial policy" *Review of Economic Studies*, 61, 197-222.

Calomiris, C. and Hubbard, R. (1990), "Firm Heterogeneity, Internal Finance and Credit Rationing", *Economic Journal*, 100, 90-104.

Calomiris, C. and Hubbard, R. (1995), "Internal Finance and Investment: Evidence from the Undistributed Profits Tax of 1936-37", *Journal of Business*, 68(4), 443-82.

Chirinko, R. and Schaller, H. (1995), "Why does liquidity matter in Investment equations?", *Journal of Money, Credit, and Banking*, 27, 527-548.

Cho, Y.D. (1996), "Financial Factors and Corporate Investment", Avebury, Ashgate.

Ciccolo, J.H. (1982), "Changing Balance Sheet Relationships in the U.S. Manufacturing Sector, 1926-1977", in *The changing roles of debt and equity in financing U.S. capital formation.* (Ed.) B.M. Friedman, University of Chicago Press, Chicago, 65-74.

Devereux, M. and Schiantarelli, F. (1990), "Investment, financial factors, and cash flow: evidence from U.K. panel data", in R. Glenn Hubbard (ed.), *Asymmetric Information, Corporate Finance and Investment* (Chicago, Chicago University Press).

Eckstein, O. and Sinai, A. (1986), "The Mechanisms of the Business Cycle in the Postwar Era", in Gordon, Robert J., [Ed.] *The American business cycle: Continuity and change*, NBER Studies in Business Cycles series, vol. 25, University of Chicago Press, 39-105.

Fazzari, S., Hubbard, R. and Petersen, B. (1988), "Financing Constraints and Corporate Investment", *Brookings Papers on Economic Activity*, 0(1), 141-95.

Friedman B.M. (1982), "Debt and Economic Activity in the United States", in *The changing roles of debt and equity in financing U.S. capital formation*, (Ed.) B.M. Friedman, University of Chicago Press, Chicago, 91-110.

Gertler, M. (1992), "Financial Capacity and Output Fluctuations in an Economy with Multiperiod Financial Relationships", *Review of Economic Studies*, 59, 455-72.

Gertler, M. and Gilchrist, S. (1994), "Monetary Policy, Business Cycles, and the Behaviour of Small Manufacturing Firms", *Quarterly Journal of Economics*, 309-340.

Gertler, M. and Hubbard, R. (1988), "Financial Factors in Business Fluctuations, in *Financial market volatility: A symposium*, Federal Reserve Bank of Kansas City Symposium Series, Kansas City, 33-71.

Greenwald, B. and Stiglitz, J. (1993), "Financial Market Imperfections and Business Cycles", *Quarterly Journal of Economics*, 108, 77-114.

Hayashi, F. (1982), "Tobins marginal Q and average Q: a neoclassical interpretation", *Econometrica*, 50, 213-224.

Hayashi, F., Inoue, T. (1991), "The relation between firm growth and Q with multiple capital goods: theory and evidence from Japanese panel data", *Econometrica*, 59, 731-753.

Holtz-Eakin, D., Newey, W. and Rosen, H. (1985), "Implementing Causality Tests with Panel Data, with an Example from Local Public Finance", National Bureau of Economic Research Technical Paper: 48.

Holtz-Eakin, D., Newey, W., and Rosen, H. (1988), "Estimating vector autoregressions with panel data", *Econometrica*, 56, 1371-1395.

Hoshi, T., Kashyap, A. and Scharfstein, D. (1991), "Corporate Structure, Liquidity, and Investment: Evidence from Japanese Panel Data", *Quarterly Journal of Economics*, 106, 33-60.

Hubbard, G. R. (1998), "Capital-Market Imperfections and Investment", *Journal of Economic Literature*, 36, 193-225.

Hubbard, G. Kashyap, A. and Whited, T. (1995), "Internal Finance and Firm Investment", *Journal of Money, Credit, and Banking*, 27, 683-701.

Jorgenson, D.W. (1971), "Econometric Studies of Investment Behaviour: a Survey", Journal of Economic Literature, 9, 1111-47.

Kashyap, A., Lamont, O. and Stein, J. (1994), "Credit Conditions and the Cyclical Behavior of Inventories", *Quarterly Journal of Economics*, 109(3), 565-92.

Kiyotaki, N. (1997), "Credit and Business Cycles", *Japanese Economic Review*, 49(1), 18-35.

Kiyotaki, N. and Moore, J. (1997), "Credit Cycles", *Journal of Political Economy*, 105(2), 211-48.

Modigliani, F. and Miller, M. (1958), "The cost of capital corporation finance, and the theory of investment", *American Economic Review*, 48, 261-297.

Myers, S. and Majluf, N. (1984), "Corporate financing and investment decisions when firms have information that investors do not have", *Journal of Financial Economics*, 13, 187-221.

Oliner, S. and Rudebusch, S. (1992), "Sources of the Financing Hierarchy for Business Investment and Agency Costs", *Review of Economics Statistics*, 74, p. 643-653.

Potter, S. (1995) "A nonlinear approach to US GNP", *Journal of Applied Econometrics*, 10, 109-125.

Schaller, H. (1990), "A re-examination of the Q-theory of investment using U.S. firm data", *Journal of Applied Econometrics*, 5, 309-325.

Schiantarelli, F. (1996), "Financial constraints and investment: methodological issues and international evidence", *Oxford Review of Economic Policy*, 12(2), 70-89.

Seth, R. (1992), "Corporate Leverage and the Business Cycle", *Contemporary Policy Issues*, 10, 65-80.

Sichel D.E.(1993), "Business cycle asymmetry: a deeper look", *Economic Inquiry*, 31, 224-236.

Stanca, L. and Gallegati, M. (1999), "The dynamic relation between financial conditions and investment: evidence from panel data", *Industrial and Corporate Change*, 8(3), 551-572.

Stiglitz, J. and Weiss, A. (1981), "Credit Rationing in Markets with Imperfect Information", *American Economics Review*, 71, 393-410.

Thoma, M. (1994), "Subsample Instability and Asymmetries in Money-Income Causality", *Journal of Econometrics*, 64 (1-2), 279-306.

Warshawsky, M. (1992), "Is There a Corporate Debt Crisis? Another Look", in G. R. Hubbard [Ed.], *Financial Markets and Financial Crises*, National Bureau of Economic Research, Chicago, University of Chicago Press.

Whited, T. (1992), "Debt, liquidity constraints, and corporate investment: evidence from panel data", *Journal of Finance*, 67, 1425-1460.

Index

MELLEN STUDIES IN ECONOMICS

1. Charles R.B. Stowe, **The Implications of Foreign Financial Institutions on Poland's Emerging Entrepreneurial Economy**
2. John P. Cochran and Fred R. Glahe, **The Hayek-Keynes Debate-Lessons for Current Business Cycle Research**
3. Heinrich Pesch, **Liberalism, Socialism and Christian Social Order,** Book 1: **The Philosophical Roots of Economic Liberalism**, translated by Rupert J. Ederer
4. Edward J. O'Boyle (ed.), **Teaching the Social Economics Way of Thinking: Selected Papers from the Ninth World Congress of Social Economics**
5. K. Brad Stamm, **Music Industry Economics: A Global Demand Model for Pre-Recorded Music**
6. Heinrich Pesch, **Liberalism, Socialism and Christian Social Order,** Book 2: **Free Market Economy or Economic Order?**, translated by Rupert J. Ederer
7. Heinrich Pesch, **Liberalism, Socialism and Christian Social Order,** Book 3: **Private Property as a Social Institution,** translated by Rupert J. Ederer
8. Heinrich Pesch, **Liberalism, Socialism and Christian Social Order,** Book 4: **The Christian Concept of the State,** translated by Rupert J. Ederer
9. Daniel Egan, **The Politics of Economic Restructuring in London, 1981-1986**
10. Stephen Gilliatt, **How the Poor Adapt to Poverty in Capitalism**
11. Luca Matteo Stanca, **The Role of Financial Markets in Generating Business Cycles**